KU-190-965

SCOTTISH POETRY 5

22 George Square, Edinburgh

North America
Aldine Publishing Company

Printed in Great Britain by
W & J Mackay & Co. Ltd, Chatham

Scottish Poetry 5

Edited by
George Bruce, Maurice Lindsay,
and Edwin Morgan
for the University Press
Edinburgh

Contents

The Shampoo. *D. M. Black*

–long des'ka?
–O not very long

little Japanese girl
prim hairstyle / precise lipstick
not out to show any emotion
if she can help it.
she clings like a fire to the clippers.
she cannot reach the top of my head
so she spends her time on the sideboards
I shall emerge like a mushroom.
one can stand a lot from a lassie

nuzzles her pleasing crotch
against my elbow
true fraternisation
I wish the shop were more empty

–shampoo 'ka?
–hai dozo.
she cranks out a vast apparatus
I hardly escape with my knees
she giggles delightedly
I feign astonishment
but of course like all men am enchanted
to be found to occupy space.
several moments
am lost in suds and fingers
pleasant oblivion
I re-surface
it is my own mad face in the mirror
and she on my shoulders
practising some sort of karate chop.

(small hope of un-tensing
this severe Scottish bone-system)
I give her a ribald grin
and she flees away shrieking with laughter
returns at once
with a hot damp towel
refreshes very lovingly
my wayworn features
I watch with extreme concentration
Kanebo's Dandy Liquid
she too with imperfect gravity
combs my hair intently
–drapes a long stretch of blue netting
onto my skull
plays on it with slapped fingers
then with a warm air from the hairdryer

–so, finish des'ka?
–hai, finish des'.
–hai domo arigato

He will be Greatly Missed. *Alan Bold*

1. Hades

Amber lighting filtered through glasses filtered
Through the smoking choke. Behind the bar a punchball
Of a face leers expectantly anxious to serve an
Arrogant pint. Heavy. Bitter. Distantly
Voices fleshed out as faces pursue a solitary
Stream of something near to thought. Brown walls.
Yellow ceiling. Multicoloured floor. And bright
Formica bar. Steady noise, stench, subject-matter.
On the wall crudely pencilled menus and specialities
Of the house. Hot unappetising pies. Beans

And the exclusive Hades sandwich. This
Is the pub called Hades. Underground, below
The road, on the corner of Hangover Street.
Movement. Endless people coming in to replace
Those going out. Predetermined activity.
The scene around a pub called Hades.

2. John

No, he is not a casualty, nor an alien of any kind
Really. Not, in fact, innately different, just
That the burgeoning bones that held his brain
Were battered from birth, systematically.
From an early age (too early for John to remember)
His mother would weekly thrust his head
Through the window, and, as he stuck there,
His father, outside, would kick the head, time
After time. It did him good, they said.
His bulging brow grew as the function
Of the contents diminished. And now
He has children of his own. They are taught
Respect for their father and, though at school
Their performances are poor, they are all
Top of every class for attendance. They have
Never missed a day, nor John a week.

3. Frederick

How Frederick became a councillor of the city
Is a long, long story. Most of it you know.
Nights puzzled out over strange logarithms,
Laboured bits of prose, syntax, and a history
That comprised dates and omitted men.
It was a sweat but, after external examinations,
Proved worthwhile. The erudition, incomplete,
Impressed his workmates and he won the respect
Of those he arched at socially. In time,

With the experience of handling men, he was
Selected for the vacant candidacy and won, with his
Pally, ever-ready smile. But underneath was
Discontent. To have got this far alone
Was to have found out why and how other men
Go further. He lifts his pint and drinks.
And frowns. He lifts his pint and drinks.

4. At Work

Clatter-pitter. Clatter-pitter. Clatter-pitter.
Steel strikes steel and oil eases the progress
Of the shining sheets of metal. Green overalls
Spotted out with oil. Grease ubiquitous, grit
Almost. From the changing-room, with its sparse
Planks of wooden floor, to the shop. Where
Eyes blink in alcoholic reminiscence. Forced
Grins and camaraderie and what one did to the wife
Last night. And the government. And the lack
Of money. In charge of the biggest machine,
Frederick. Glowing, scrubbed, maliciously
Happy. Outwith the circle of the shop,
John. Doomed to sweep up and tidy for the rest.
Resentful, dark, brooding. From his sulk
A line to the effervescent Frederick. The
Most intolerable of all. Clatter-pitter.

5. At Home

Chop go the jaws, and chop chop
The family muscles. John eats first,
After saying a brief prayer, and stares
At the rented television in the focal
Corner of the room. Mrs. John says nothing
And the kids the same. Action is invoked
When interference on the set intrudes.
John with well-developed expertise adjusts

The switchboard on the back, he is a
Pilot, a computer operator, everything
At once. Entertainment cut off, he turns
To the children and blames with blows
Their acquiescence in this act. The wife
Says nothing, but to quiet the noise, she
Potters with the washing in the sink.
In the absence of the children knits and looks.

6. At Rest

Tonight a brief hello at home, shared
With his older cousin, then Frederick walks
Briskly to the football ground. Floodlights
Bathing the grass in luminosity, the bright
Ball passing from foot to practised foot.
The teams in red and green and Frederick knows
Their names. He squeezes into the area
Behind the red goalkeeper and waits for green goals.
He sees green, he sees the green jerseys glowing,
He sees the grass reject the red. He throws
His green scarf round his reddish neck. He
Whistles green whistles, shouts green shouts.
He makes the passes in his head, anticipates
The goals. His face is flushed, red, almost
Purplish, with the rivulets of blood.
He breathes with difficulty. Pants.

7. The Match

Green ball to green. The nippy winger
Gets past one, past two, past FOUL!
Down and writhing and a surge of moral
Indignation sweeps the green-scarved end
Of the stand. FOUL! PENALTY! But
No, the referee is firm and it's a free
Kick. Green ball to green but FOUL!

Again! He says play on, but nippy winger
Still on ground is hurt. He then gets up.
He throws a green-raged punch at a red
Belly. The whistle goes. The match is done.
ROBBED! WE WERE ROBBED! A goal-less draw
On paper, but, to the green-scarves, a two-nil
Victory. And nippy winger has his name taken.
The beercans fly and flash in gold, in golden red,
And smack onto the pitch. Beer dribbles out.

8. The Departure

John has had his flesh for the evening.
He has lashed out, thrust in, and is well.
Straight to Hades. He gets dressed, and
Ponderously stumbles along to his favourite bar.
He'd like to know the score. The set broke
Down. Behind the bar a voice explains the match
Is hardly over, and that they all will know
The score when it pours out. John tells the bar
It should have the telly, his remarks addressed to
All. No one disagrees. He sets them up. Three,
Four, five whiskies, the liquid thick and clinging
To the minute glass that threatens to shatter
In his hand. I'll wash them down with beer,
He says, and beer is served. John then decides
To go through it again, and spends his wages.
Frederick enters in green. John sees red.

9. The Discussion

John sees red as Frederick comes in green.
ROBBED! He downs a beer. The score,
He says, there was no score. We should
Have had two goals, but no. Two penalties
Were due to us, but no. Two certain goals,
But no. Frederick is not pleased. John

Laughs. For once the ref was fair, he grins.
Fair? The ref fair? Frederick asks him.
What do you know about being fair? You thick
Uncultured brutish man, you weren't at the match.
You couldn't tell a football from a frog. You
Exercise the right of frothing your foolish
Opinions forth. You're fit for finding fault
With first-class players, my behind. As for the red,
The replay will see them a mess, like you.
Ha! You leave, you've no reply. A pint.

10. Determination

Into the black street, whirling with the lights
John lunges. The words like blows still pummel
At his head. He staggers forward and stumbles.
And holds his hurting head. He sways and when
He turns sees only light and blinding dark.
Thump thump thump hits his heart and his fists
Come together and crack each other. He howls
His horror at the wind and gets his knees up from
The ground. Cars screech past and laughter mocks
Him from below. His neck, like putty, sways
Around. His feet unsteady on the street. Eyelids
Compress and brow bears pain. Teeth crush
Together. He runs towards the nearest lane and
Leans against a wall. Still the words beat against
The blood inside him. Still the mocking voice
Hurts. He lifts his arm and roars. Louder.

11. Conflict

Furiously Frederick walks home. His belly
Full of beer is unprepared for the pistoning it
Gets. Down, he can see the bulk of John and
Feel his pounding fists flailing at his face.
Stop, he tries to cry. But silently the blackness

Overwhelms him. Stop, John cries to himself, but
On and on the thumping hams persist.
Frederick's visage is a mess like afterbirth,
His blood goggles in thick blobs. Even
In the dark it sounds like lava, looks
Like beetroot with the juice. The rotund
Frame twitches and then stops. The brain
No longer in command loses the pulses.
And John knows fear, halts and screams.
His father in his head is kicking him. His
Memories are vivid as they haven't been for years.

12. Obituary

A forty-nine-year old city councillor was
Brutally beaten to death last night near
His home. The attack took place around
Midnight and police are holding a forty-
Year-old manual worker for questioning.
The body was found by an officer on night
Duty. In his six years of service Frederick
R. was identified with his party's ambitious
Programme of modernising the roads. His
Municipal victory was taken to mark
A revival in the fortunes of the party at
Local level. Perhaps his greatest single
Achievement was in convincing his colleagues
That council members be allowed a free vote
On all matters pertaining to the welfare of
The city. He will be greatly missed.

Couch-Grass. *Derek Bowman*

Couch-grass is a no-nonsense grass.
Cuts tubes through clay, tilts bricks,
  Advances in phalanxes,
    Spears docks.

Quitch-grass is a live-wire grass.
Half-a-chance, soil's quick with it:
  Mesh your hand down in a mass,
    —Taut net.

Couch-grass is a rat-race grass.
Uses its nous–sweet smile, bear-hug
  —Takes over the whole patch,
    Top dog.

Quitch-grass is a Realpolitik grass.
If you want to get on, act tough.
  Elbow your way through! Lash out!
    The rough stuff!

Rhubarb in Spring. *Derek Bowman*

Pink negro finger-tips grope
Up out of winey wood
That coffined them. Membranes
Dome, burst. Free the green bubble
And squeak of glossy folds
Tight involved as walnut-brains.
Uprears their stem of flesh
To set the teeth on edge,
Purge and seed as trees.

They say rhubarb graces the graves
Of Balkan peasantry, moustachioed,
Conspiratorial, the breed that murders
Royalty in open leather-buttoned cars
And, grinning wide, sets all in ferment.
Or did rheum once bless Christendom
As huge and veiny baldaquins
Swaying monstrously, stalking cardinal
Red the earth, when all was swamp?

Houses. *George Bruce*

1. Suddenly our house went up in the air.
The slates, rafters, chimneypots, masonry
burst out like a gust of starlings
and stopped 30 feet up.
They then decided to come down again.

That was in 1941.
I believed my mother was inside.

2. In Edinburgh houses come down.

Without giving notice the cement balcony
of a council house left its assigned
position
and made a new map on the pavement.

3. Our house is different; it is very old,
it creaks a bit in the wind,
is water-tight now and then,
comfortable for mice with good runways:
it should do my time.

Quixote in a Windmill. *George Bruce*

He saw it hoisting itself from salt marshes
into his trembling sky. It stood
on the edge of water-meadows turning
to marram grass to sand only
and then shallow pale sea.

He looked at the broken webs
that cracked but did not move.
Once this castle was his when
the wind bawled about, the sails
whirled in the turmoil of his mind;

racketing, squealing, grinding, they became
his madness: he watched his brain lifted
to the brazen sky, thrown down on stones—
he was King for a howling winter
till the soft Spring came and flowers.

Autobiography. *George Bruce*

For years
a schoolmaster looked over my right shoulder
in case my punctuation went wrong.

For years
a minister looked over my left shoulder
in case I committed a moral solecism.

They've gone.
Now I watch the sparrows in the green grass.
'Lechers!'

Reflection at Sixty. *George Bruce*

Thunder knocks about the house,
tries doors and windows.
Night.   I listen in bed.

Somewhere around
there's a birth going on
that concerns me.
At Bridlington Spa
my wax moustachioed purple uncle
used to sway in the salted breeze.

'Give it up,' he said,
'All this bother about meaning.
Douse lights and out.'

And Our Gifts to the Seasons. *Thomas Clark*

he went out
   the snow was hard packed
   stale

'to be unmoved'
   he thought
the wind blew everything
   in its path
'to be unmoved'

there was a summer
   lilies grew
   in great profusion
he lay down along the bank
   and she lay also
   they listened
   to the water to their own

silence
'let me come in to you'
lilies moving on the bank

the road now
out of town
was difficult
picking one's way
in the deep snow
'there was a time
I'd have turned from
this senseless ordinance'
but no return
the sleigh was there
he felt
that dark strength flowing
from the horses

(he heard her laugh)

and his the only footprints
traced upon the snow

Clyde Water. *Thomas Clark*

the swallow has broken
free from the grand mass
hovers directly
above without movement
one ship comes in
nets full of words
all shouting 'open'
the sky gets real red

Over the Moors : March. *Thomas Clark*

elbow against the sky
a warrior is sleeping on the land
arms folded to his breast
he is easy with the seasons
head almost lolling
into the Celtic sea

before spring
burned old tree trunks
fence posts burned and toppling

a Roman wall
exploded across the hills
grey stones brown stones blue stones
tough old
grass jutting through

my friends were eager
to say everything at once
I told them
head south and be warm
and be free and talk easily

spring will come
when the fires are low

On Craigie Hill. *Stewart Conn*

The old farmhouse seems centuries ago:
The steadings slouched under a sifting of snow
For weeks on end, lamps hissing, logs stacked
Like drums in the shed, the ice having to be cracked
To let the shaggy cats drink. Or
Back from the mart through steaming pastures
Men would come riding—their best
Boots gleaming, rough tweeds pressed
To a knife-edge, pockets stuffed with notes.

Before that even, I could visualise (from coloured
Prints) traps rattling, wheels spinning; furred
Figures posing like sepia dolls
In a waxen world of weddings and funerals.
When Todd died, last of the old-stagers,
Friends of seventy years followed the hearse.
Soon the farm went out of the family: the Cochranes
Going to earth or, like their cousins,
Deciding it was time to hit town.

The last link broken, the farm-buildings stand
In a clutter below the quarry. The land
Retains its richness—but in other hands.
Kilmarnock has encroached. It is hard to look
Back with any sense of belonging:
Too much has changed, is still changing.
This blustery afternoon on Craigie Hill
I regard remotely the muddy track
My father used to trudge along, to school.

Smell of my Father's House. *Lindsay Cooper*

smell of my father's house
strange
after only a year

lamplit gusts
polish the road
cyclist in a yellow cape

pause for the fool moon
wet footsteps
echoing

autumn gust
flying leaves
paper birds

late night
still light
hot chips

crooked cupboard door
my room is tired
sinking in this old building

tired
drunk
pissing in the sink

trapped moth
makes the room
small

sly
ingratiating
feeding the landladies children

Forecast for a Quiet Night. *Robin Fulton*

a secret cone will drop in Rothiemurcus
causing not the slightest local disturbance

a quiet wind will stroke Loch Araich-linn—
an indiscretion no-one can possibly notice

by dawn imperceptible frosty wrinkles
will have puckered the edges of countless backwaters

by dawn too a generation of mice
will have been snipped by a night-shift of owls
working separately and almost in silence

and the mild local disturbance behind the eyes
of the invalid
will have been noted only by the next of kin

Laying Up. *Robin Fulton*

at a signal dead leaves hop
stumble fan out across the putting green
like squeaky children in a speeded up film
jerkily spreading out from school

nature is comic,
we lap up our feelings more calmly

each of our five senses is wrapped in clean
newspaper and set on a dry shelf

in winter light
even the dullest stones are luminous
and so we settle holding ourselves stone-still

Leave-takings. *Robin Fulton*

1. the frozen grass snaps and tinkles
the skyline barely divides
darkness above and darkness beneath

he turns out of his own shadow
opens his many-coloured coat
and offers me an array of spices,

a little warmth a sharp taste
of sin in the season of ice
pastel glints of salvation,
I savour a few and watch the gold
sign of the fish dangle at his throat—
and say no

2. all the traffic signs have withered
the fields are black the last fires
of the last wrecks smother themselves

he is cutting the night open
he stares ahead eyeing the curve
of a scimitar, his lights finger
the dead parts swept to the verge

he offers me (without condition)
this lethal beauty that is his

to survive when the motorways curl
like burning paper, when fly-overs
crumple and melt, to outlive
the cars that disembowel each other

his driving-seat is a soft throne
I touch his golden steering-wheel—
and say no

3. in the desert then saying no

the hermit lives by a holy well
sunk in his dry imagination
he draws spilling cupfuls of images

he pours grass over the sand
poppies drip from his wet fingers
he wakes girls from sleeping stoncs
sweet perfumes of crushed plants

they all drain away in the sand
but he smiles and offers me a seed
from one of his everlasting trees

I roll the hard seed on my palm
never to be at the will of the rocks
never to suffer the grey silence
and the seed in my hand is a cut jewel—
and I say no

4. she must have been young once, the wine
is sour she says

I follow her in and take my place
among the photos and carved ivory
and the furniture no-one would want

but she has singled me out she says
the wine is sour yet here is a little
that somehow survived us all
here is a curious phial of my youth

I hold it up to the dusty light
I think of the miles and the beads of ice
dead fingers dead eyes

and painfully
I say no

Invitations. *Robin Fulton*

he
invited me into his lungs

he promised I'd find an old beehive
in a spring garden coming into bloom
with only an occasional staggering bee
that mumbles now and again obscure messages

I said No thanks
I admire their habits
but I don't trust bees
and my own constitution
is full of obscure mumblers

but I did visit his head
and climbed a giddy ladder to his topmost attic
which was dry and warm and contained only
a box pasted with pictures of an old war
(in mine are bundles of letters I shouldn't have kept)

I found a window he told me was not there
I inspected the world from an astonishing angle

when I came back he was upset to see me,
most people who visited the attic he said
became like lost children and couldn't get down

I knew that when he had recovered his composure
he would invite me into his digestive tract

The Big Music. *Robert Garioch*

And, ten to wan the piper is a cockney. Hugh MacDiarmid

Victoria Street in London, the place gaes wi the name,
a Hanoverian drill-haa, near Buckingham Palace,
near the cross-Channel trains, Edinburgh coaches,
Army and Navy Stores, an ex-abbey, a cathedral,
near the Crazy Gang, the Windsor, Artillery Mansions,
no faur, owre the water, frae the Lambeth Walk,
near the exotic kirk-spire carved wi the Stars and Stripes,
disappointed nou, a frustum, whangit wi a boomb.
This great Victorian drill-haa is naethin like Scotland,
binna the unco hicht and vastness of the place.
The judges jouk into their tent; the piper treads the tarmac.
His gear leams in the sunlicht of hunner-and-fifty-watt suns,
while we in the crowd luik on, MacAdams and Watts wi the lave.
Skinklan and pairticoloured, the piper blaws life in his wind-cod,
aefald, ilka pairt in keeping, the man, his claes and the pipes,
in keeping wi this place, as tho he stuid in Raasay,
Alaska, India, Edinburgh Castle, of coorse, for that maitter,
like a traivler I met in the rain on the Cauld Stane Slap, and him dry;
like the Big Rowtan Pipe itself, that can mak its ain conditions,
as the blaw-torch brenns under water in its ain oxygen-bell,
like the welder's argon island, blawn in the thick of the air,
sae the piper blaws his ain warld, and tunes it in three octaves,
a steil tone grund on the stane, and shairpit on the ile-stane,
like a raisit deil, mair inexorable nor onie ither music,
for the piper cannae maister this deevil of the reeds,
binna to wirry him aathegither, and brek the spell.
Nou, jaggit as levin, a flash of notes frae the chanter
slaps throu the unisoun, and tines itsel in the drones,
no jist richtlie in tune; the snell snarl dirls wi a beat,
sae the piper eases the jynts of the drones, and tries again,
and again, and again, he fettles the quirks of his fykie engine,
flings the fireflaucht of melody, tined an octave abuin the drones,

bass drone and twa tenor drones geynear in tune on A,
wi a michtie strang harmonic bummlan awa on E,
that the piper is ettlan to lock deid-richt in tune wi the chanter,
for the pipes are a gey primitive perfected instrument
that can fail a fine piper whiles, as his art may fail,
tho it warks in the tradition of John MacKay of Raasay,
guardit throu generations of teachers and learners and teachers,
and thon piper staunds forenenst us, skeelie in mind and body,
wi the sowl, a mystery greater nor mind and body thegither,
that kythes itsel by virr of its presence or absence in music.
Yet piper or pipes may fail, whan the piper wad be at his best,
ane of his reeds no jist richt, ae finger no swipper or souple,
the strang rule of the will my fankle, and tine the rhythm;
for aa that, comes the time whan the mind, body and sowl
and the reeds, the fowreteen sections, the sheepskin wind-cod
seasoned inside wi honey, or wi some patent concoction,
whan the piper and pipes in sympathy ken that the nicht is the nicht,
as Smooth John MacNab bragged on a very different occasion,
sae the piper, his pipes, judges, the warld at lairge
aa gree, yince, for a wunner, that a piobaireachd is pleyed richt.
Nae artist wad hae his medium onie itherweys ordert.
And aa this time my thocht gaes wannerin its lane,
in a three-octave chaos naukit binna its ain harmonics,
a state whaur aa things are possible, and naethin luiks very likely.
Doctor Johnson likit the pipes, we're aye tellt, because he wes deif;
for my pairt I think, like the Shah, wha likit the first tune best,
he kennd music whan he heard it, whan it garred his nervestrings dirl.
I mind, yince, masel, I mainaged near eneuch the great drone
to hear a gey guid-gaun piobaireachd, aye, and to smell it anaa:
I cuidnae mak up my mind, wes it Talisker or Laphroaig;
I jalousit a Westeren maut guffan out, maist musical.
Nou, huge, in tune, our stane-and-airn glen
dirls three octaves, A in unisoun.
Strange hou this music has nae begin or end;
even the tuning, tho nae pairt of the tune,
langs to the music, as duis the tune itself,

sae that the *urlar*, grund of the hale thing,
taks place insensibly as daith or life.
Pacing fu slawlie, wi steidie meisured mairch,
the piper blaws the lang bare notes of his lament,
a tune that bides lang jist twa steps frae the tap
of the chanter's scale, sae heich that it maun faa,
no faur; it rises, syne faas ferder, in dool,
lifts its heid twice: the cadence ends the tune.
The slaw, waesom melody, returning owre and owre,
wi smaa, clever cheenges, that keep our senses keen,
the cadence eith-kennd, airtan aathin in time,
comes like sad nicht, that ends ilk dowie day.
The piper hauds on, with the siccarness of doom,
fowre centuries of culture ruggan at his hairt
like the michtie pressure tearing throu his reeds,
hauds on til his time, wi the richtness of art,
that is no semplie richt, but we feel that it is richt.
The theme birls slawlie, and aye as it wins roun,
the neist variorum adds on its ain device,
mair short notes and mair, that garr the dirgie daunce;
the aureat lament lowes mair and mair wi pride,
till there is nae note, but loups it wi the lave,
tho, wi the music loupin, the piper nou staunds still.
Here comes the unco ferlie of the pipes,
the first of the grace-notes, like a precious stane,
gale-force music, delicately ruled,
a thrawn, strang Clydesdale; the horseman kens the word.
Allanerlie the great Hieland pipe can mak this soun,
this rattle of reedy noise, the owretones brattlan thegither,
wi maybe a swirlan danger, like musardrie of maut.
Piobaireachd adorns tragedy wi maist seensie jewels.
Men, dour as quartz, responsive as quartz to licht,
mak this shairp intellectual and passionat music,
dangerous, maist dangerous, and naethin moderat,
florischan in the warld, a dauntless form of life.

The piobaireachd comes til an end, gin we may cry it end,
the grund naukit again, as tho it had aye been sae.
Gin it werenae a competition, wi international rules,
there seems nae reason why it suidnae stert owre again,
if the piper has braith eneuch, and there seems nae dout about that,
but he neatly thraws the thrapple of the deil in his pipes,
that dies decently, wi nae unseemly scrauch.
He taks leave of us wi dignity, turns, and is gane.
The judges rate him heich, but no in the first three.

Bingo! Saith the Lord. *Robert Garioch*

Ye ken of bingo-haas, I suldna wunner;
aabody's heard of sin. Tho ye may scunner
to hae yer lugs filled wi its nestie name,
ye'll hear eneuch about it, jist the same
Scotland itsel, whase folk suid be mair worth
Gode's grace nor onie ither race on earth,
gambles on Bingo. Our guid toun anaa,
even Dreepdaily, had its Bingo-haa.
Had it, indeed: it doesnae hae it nou,
praise the Lord's mercies, tho they be but few.
Bingo's aa richt for thaim that are haufe-cracked,
but no the Scots, certes, forsooth in fact!
And niver sall be, while I hae the job
of bylin Scotland's conscience on my hob,
elect and walit by a special grace,
alane to guaird the weilfare of the race,
a michtie scourge for mediocre hides,
especially the backsliders' backsides.
Hou can a Scotsman worthy of the name
waste aa his time upon this wicked game?
Hou can a Scot, whase thochts suid be on Hevin,
think mair of Kellie's Ee or Legs Eleeven?

Duis yon free Scot, member of this Free Kirk,
mind of his forebears skulking in the mirk
to get a shot at Tam Dalziel's dragoons?
No him—he's owre taen-up wi his cuppoons.
But that's anither maitter; I forgot.
Aweill, som puir denationalisit Scot,
I niver mainaged to find out jist wha,
stertit this craze to hae a Bingo-haa.
I cuidnae stap them: our degenerate sons
floatit a company to raise their funds,
got them anaa, tho nae bank wad advance
a loan to clear the dry-rot frae the manse,
and sae thay got their haa, in spite of me,
cockit upon a cleuch abuin the sea,
a bit of Anglo-Scots vulgarity
biggit of London brick and blasphemy,
so there stuid Gode and I, we saw richt weill,
by virr surrendert til the Anglo-Deil.
I didnae hide it, I wes vexit sair,
but if ye've heard I opent fire wi prayer
as tho it were a gun, ye've heard a lee;
prayer maun aye be yaised wi charity;
forbye, I wadnae claim a parity
wi Moses, for ensample, eh, na, na,
they cannae say I did it. Still, yon haa,
wi aa its Bingoists, gaed owre the cleuch
in a gey stormy sea, that's richt eneuch,
bit it's no true that, as it tummelt in,
the hale Kirk-Session cried out, 'Lord, weil duin!'

Progress. *Duncan Glen*

Is not nature wonderful

The goose walks oot and gets its mither
baith schooled and weel conditioned

Is not nature wonderful

We cam oot heid first – get a slap
and oor mither tongue

Is not nature wonderful

They gae walkin oot ane ahint the ither

Is not nature wonderful

Hush a bye baby on a tree top
A wash and sang and then to sleep

Is not progress wonderful

Ane and ane maks twa
And Jack gaes up the hill

Is not progress wonderful

Jack. Jack. Jack.
That's my guid boy.
Thief. Thief. Thief.
Jack. Jack. Jack.
That's my guid boy.

Is not progress wonderful

And soon in fine condition for schoolin

Is not progress wonderful

And the goose walks oot and gets
a box on a string.

Is not nature wonderful

Relatives. *Duncan Glen*

aw's on the move

tak a tree
tak a rose
tak an auld grey mare
tak a nierembergia
tak me

and God made the warld
Monday to Setterday
—and sat back on Sunday

tak a flooer in a lapel
tak the licht o TV
tak climbin clematis
tak Bach at the organ
tak you playin us
tak then
tak noo
tak me as you
aw's in the move
till we put in
the mind

sittin back on Sunday

and yet and yet
the mind kens itsel best
—better

aw's on the move
tak a coffin cairrit oot shouther high
tak an actor on the boards
tak the meenister in his goon
tak the bride in white

aw's on the move
oot there in here

aw's on the move
aw's my relatives

aw's in the poetry

Return of the Fishing Boats, Schull. *Giles Gordon*

At night, the fishing boats return.
Without sound, they approach the pier,
their engines silenced by the sea.
The wash of the waves is not heard
—nor listened to: it is absorbed
into the pace of the village.
Each of the five boats is emptied
of its still breathing silver fruit.

Waiting lorries drive with the fish
through the night to the big city.
The pier is empty of people
—of fishermen, boys, visitors.
The last car has driven away.
The five boats, tucked against the pier
(two on each side, one at the end),
prop up the village as it sleeps.

Penitence. *Andrew Greig*

I have a picture in my mind
that will not sleep

Orpheus padding silently through the grey
halls of the underworld

opening huge oak doors
and slipping through
like a dusky pigmy
the dissolving arch ways
fell in smoke behind him
and the length of his penitence
was 7 years

The halls of Dis are as a tomb
wherein the body's gone

He sometimes thought
of musical rain drumming
an even percussion
on the cobbled streets
outside the tavern
where he treasured in dalliance
a long winter's length

Orpheus the caretaker
searching the halls of Dis

Orpheus the silent porter
learning how to weep

Sarcophagus. *Robin Hamilton*

This stone rests on Caesar: leader of legions,
Man of might, who would have lifted it
Had he been alive. Now this stone
Is a closed lid upon Caesar, man of might,
Leader of legions, now dead.

But which Caesar? All led legions, and all
Were men of might, according to the court
Poets (at least in their official verses:
For private circulation, they were more scurrilous,
But no more truthful—the liars!)

Nero we remember, the mad fiddler—
But his tomb would be of calcined marble,
Fired brick, words cut with silver chisels.

Or one who died at Ravenna, of
The plague.

Or the seven apocryphal founders.
The first and most apocryphal, who was
A god. The last and least apocryphal,
Who was a tyrant.

Caesar or Kaiser. Across the sea,
The names change, legion to horde,
Wine to beer, marble to granite,
But still Caesar, war leader,
Stone lifter, lying with withered hams
In a box with a stone lid.

Los Angeles Poem. *Robin Hamilton*

And as she walked, the white silk scarf
Slid down her golden hair.

And still she talked, all unaware
Of the still hand that stroked her hair.

Gravity, daring as greatly as he dared
Had kissed her scarf but not her hair.

Ambrose Manson. *Roderick Hart*

Somewhere the sun, was in a sky of its
own brightness and its blinding stones,
in the sand and the candent sea
by which he walked

when Ambrose came from the stalk-still
marram-grass, from the tale he told
like the town bell, and those old footprints
from his other small beginnings

to the cobbled streets where their procession was;
they saw him waiting in the heat, his eyelids
heavy as the thoughts he kept them on,
closed against the opening of the gate

and took his hands to ring their careless carillon:
birds hung hot in the air, when they came walking
threadbare through the blue-bright day, the old
he must ring in, and out the new.

sandals opened on their toes;   weathered nails
driven and grown in the tree-foot wood
sprang to the tread those measuring monks
steadied as they went staff-handed on,

and did not Kate in the coach they ushered in
allow her genial jester from its spare-boned ribs
light on his cork-soled shoes, lead
the small feet following away—

this once a year when she appeared to be herself
she had not shown him, her in her different greatness
a finity of objects, a finity of answers,
Ambrose' open eyes and his pleasure,

down the heat-hazed herringway they strode
he'd paced them straight and dead,
red his eye in the salt
of a narrowed noon.

the boats were gone; the men
it dawned upon who saw the tide,
its height, the wet weed slap the
stone in the half-right light

had left the berths a wide gift in their wake;
he pent his heaven on their mending nets and
let his fullness word in the earless air.
the rope handless, the bell unrung

the sunlight westered where the circles met
ago between the hidden fleet and eye,
and then the gate can shut.
their second twilight this;

he'd see the bound boats homeward soon,
hear the pier ring to the fishermen's feet.
the crates unslung, the catch without the
bread would be enough.

Praises. *Alan Jackson*

let us praise the condition of the onion:
the onion does not drive the motor car
the onion does not go to the place of work
the onion does not enter into union with unpredictable creatures
but the onion can be destroyed—by disease or damp.
let us then praise disease and damp
and, since they are separate things,
let us praise them separately.
let us praise damp first:
damp can destroy almost anything
damp is great
but damp can be kept out
and damp can be destroyed—by fire or heat.
let us, for the sake of argument, call fire and heat the same thing
and let us praise them—it, and damp-proof walls:
damp-proof walls are great.
but they can be destroyed—by fire.
let us therefore praise fire twice:
fire is great great.
but fire can be kept out
and fire can be destroyed—by damp.
let us therefore praise damp again, it and fire-proof walls:
they are great.
but let us now rather praise disease
which was to be praised after damp in the first place:
disease can destroy any living thing
disease is great
but it cannot destroy any dead thing.
let us therefore praise all dead things:
they do not drive the motor car
they do not go to the place of work
they do not enter into union with unpredictable creatures
but, also, they do not grow in the dark ground

they do not suit themselves in golden skins
and they do not make us cry when we come into them.

let us therefore, finally, praise the condition of the onion.

Da Waanderin Folk. *Peter Jamieson*

Raggit bit a canvas,
—Wi' LK still veev apon hit—
Riggit apon twa poles
Naar da aald moss-grown daek.

Fur shaltir diss wis braa,
Da duggit girss kovvrd wi' strae
Medd a fine flaatchi fur da bairns,
Sleepy, hungry, oon-wyshin, bit happy at dir ploy,
—Wha sall ken whit skru da strae wis frae—
Guid feth, does hit raelly maetter?

Naar da tent openin a lowin fire
—Dir nae waant a paets i da hill—
Nae maetter wha's tushkar kiust dem.

Wi' a stewin-pot hingin frae tree bits a iron.

Da man beetlin awa apo tin,
Da wife on 'ir hookirs aaber fur gin.

On da daek a peerie wran
'Cheep, cheepd!', sam's spaekin ta da boddies.
A half-nyaakit boy laachs
An scoarns da burd,
Is he rinns ower ta da rinklin burn
An demmels wi' a bucket.

Transplant. *William Keys*

Sometimes black against the sun
I see the man
Coming towards me his face
Obscured carrying water
One hand he holds out to me
And I shrink towards him
Pleading Please Don't Don't
Hurt me Please Leave me
Offering myself.

Sometimes with his eyes piercing
The sun and his face obscured
I see the man
He doesn't know my name
But he can find me anywhere
He offers water
He doesn't follow me he's
Just there always in the right
Place to find me.

Sometimes in the night
With his light killing my eyes
I see the man
I move and he moves and
We move together I hold
Out my cup to him he gives
Me to drink I take his water
It burns my throat
He knows my tastes.

Storie di Cristo. *Colin Kirkwood*
14th century paintings by Paolo da Venezia

1. This is a hollow mountain,
a tent.
In it a cradle and in it the baby,
shining.
A cow is licking his right arm.
A donkey is licking his left ear.
The audience is wearing crowns, halos, wings,
or at least praying.
He's got his eye on the cow.

2. Jesus up to his chest in green water.
Red-haired John the baptist
reaches a skinny arm from the bank
to touch his head. Towards it
a pigeon bombing straight down
from the blue sun.
Talk about vertical take-off!

3. Jesus looks worried at the head of the table
(halo bigger than the rest).
He's got a hand on John's shoulder.
Eleven of the twelve have halos.
They're looking at him, or at each other,
worriedly.
Judas is sitting on a stool,
not on the bench like the rest.
No halo, hair uncombed,
reaching for a piece of bread or fish.
He looks at Jesus, feeling: *he knows.*

4. All the helmeted soldiers
   are watching Judas kiss Jesus
   but the eyes of these two
   have flicked left:
   Peter is sawing off this bloke's ear.

5. Jesus carries the cross effortlessly
   flashing a worried glance
   back at his mother
   —who's gone all emotional
   wringing her hands.
   The man behind her son
   wearing a black dagger
   shoves her out of the road.

6. Small angels swarming round the cross,
   one is catching the blood in a bowl.
   Jesus' eyes are shut.
   One of the soldiers is pointing up at him solemnly,
   and he has a halo.
   The rest of them look neutral
   like people at the pictures.
   But on the left
   one of the women has stabbed herself
   with a big sword!

7. The soldiers are sleeping.
   An angel is standing in the empty coffin.
   Mary is asking the gardener:
   where's the body?

8. This is the happy ending, supposed to be.
   Jesus in a big egg
   carried by angels
   in mid-air . . .
   head bent
   looking down worriedly
   at the people on the ground
   looking up at him
   worriedly.

Storie di Cristo. *Colin Kirkwood*

Other paintings of the same period

1

There are several of the crowning of the virgin
in which Jesus and Mary are side by side on a throne.
Both heads are bent
in pity-love towards each other,
but Mary's is more bent.
Her curvy form looks boneless.
I guess her lord is saying:
keep it up dear, you're doing a grand job,
look, d'you mind if I leave you the dishes tonight,
there's a bloke I promised to wake from the dead . . . .
Lutes, flutes, and xylophones
sound all round.

2

A man sitting on a throne in mid-air,
presumably God. He looks serious.
Down below, lots of skeletons
laughing happily,
holding little red books in their hands.
Mao wasn't the first.

The Good Thief. *Tom Leonard*

heh jimmy
yawright ih
stull wayz urryi
ih

heh jimmy
ma right insane yirra pape
ma right insane yirwanny uz jimmy

see it nyir eyes
wanny uz

heh

heh jimmy
lookslik wirgonny miss thi gemm
gonny miss thi GEMM jimmy
nearly three a cloke thinoo

dark init
good jobe theyve gote thi lights

Words, for E. *Tom Leonard*

The sky is blue, or something. Anyway, it's there.
Your words are hands, stroking me, stroking the sky,
Blue sky, names, people. It's marvellous. I'm king,
And your words are a line of ships. The guns fire.
Blue sky, names, people. I take the salute.

You are beautiful, sometimes. Now.
I feel for words for you. The ship rising, falling,
The horizon, a line rising, falling, behind your hair.
Words rise, spray. I like to think of you as giving
Structure. A gentleness. A constancy.

Simile Please / Say Cheese. *Tom Leonard*

as the sea comes ogling ogling up the sand
and drops down its hankie of seaweed for the land to hand over

but the land doesn't bother for the land still fancies the sky
and the sea goes away in the huff but it always comes back

like a small man standing at the bottom of Big Ben holding a long
thread tied to the top

which slowly bends over as the man creeps furtively away

only the clock tower has been secretly made of rubber which straightens
up to hurl the man away up to Scotland

only the man has been secretly made of Scottish rubber so that he
bounces to his feet amang his ain folk

darling . . .

The Other Side of the Ticket. *Tom Leonard*

I have quoted the number of deaths in obscure battles
In order to pass examinations; I have quoted the number
Of deaths in more recent disasters, that some life might be
Brought to a dying conversation; I have been moved by
Animated discussions in restaurants on the question of
World famine; I have shuffled in anxious queues that
Could not wait to see the authentic films of the tortured
Under the Nazi rule, and I have listened to the satisfied
Shocked voices, and agreed that it was terrible to watch;
I have fled from pacifists, beside themselves with rage;
I have befriended people with or without pamphlets and
Badges, whose logic would hammer its fist on the table,
Or announce itself in a rush of words when an innocent
Topic was introduced: I have watched them fumbling along
Their narrow lanes, scrawling on the huge brick walls
On either side that God is love, or that God does not exist

At all, or whatever the motto transcribed from the gleam
In their eyes. But I have laughed, being myself for once,
On having picked up a newspaper with its frantic reasons for
Despair, joy, or natural pride, and having realised that
Only the crossword had changed from the previous day.
And bored with sincerity, the drunkard's tight grip on the
Lapel, I have returned to the Nazi film to jeer at the
Wide-eyed crowds, and been thrown out, clutching
My ticket that thanked me and asked me to come again.

An Elegy. *Maurice Lindsay*
Matthew Lindsay : 1884/1969

You might have died so many kinds of death
as you drove yourself through eighty-four Novembers—

1916. The Cameronian officer
keeping the Lewis guns he commanded chattering
over the seething mud, that the enemy
should be told only in terms of bulky bodies,
for which, oak leaves, a mention in dispatches.

1918. The fragment of a shell
leaving one side of a jaw and no speech,
the bone graft from the hip, Shakespeare mouthed
(most of the others asserting silences)
over and over again, till the old words
shaped themselves into audibility.

1921. An eighty-per-cent
disability pension, fifty the limit of life
expectancy, a determination of courage
that framed the public man, the ready maker
of witty dinner speeches, the League of Nations,
the benefits of insurance, the private man
shut in his nightly study, unapproachable,

sufficient leader of sporting tournaments,
debates, and the placing of goodwill greetings in clubs.

1935. Now safely past
the doctors' prophecies. Four children, a popular
outward man wearing maturity,
top of his business tree, when the sap falters
and the soon-to-be-again confounded doctors
pronounce a world-wide cruise the only hope,
not knowing hope was all he ever needed
or counted on to have to reckon with.

1940 to 50. Wartime fears
not for himself but for his family,
the public disappointments and the private
disasters written off with stock quotations
from Shakespeare or FitzGerald, perhaps to show
the well-worn commonness of experience,
the enemy across the mud, old age.

1959. It was necessary
at seventy-five, to show he couldn't be taken
by enfilading weaknesses. A horse
raised his defiance up. It threw him merely
to Russia on a stretcher, with two sticks
to lean beginner's Russian upon.

1969. The end of a decade
of surgeons, paling blindness, heart attacks
all beaten with familiar literature
bent into philosophic platitudes,
to the January day in his dressing-gown
when he sat recording plans for a last Burns Supper—

You might have died so many kinds of death
as you drove yourself through eighty-four Novembers
till you fell from your bed, apologised for such foolishness,
and from your sleep rode out where no man goes.

Games Mistress. *Maurice Lindsay*

Always, and for its own sake, the game!
There was no other way for healthy girls
to win their colours in the trials ahead
(necessarily unspecified beyond the
boundaries of school hymn and hockey pitch).
Generations careering towards this goal
coached from the side by her antiseptic figure,
upright as discipline, forwarding the game
that left her changeless on the cheering line,
carbolically safe from loving's germs—

breath's taste in the kiss
against a hard-pressed door;
the steamed-up hand in the car
loosening motor senses;
the public bromide wedding
harvesting honeymoon;
legs arched for the trawl
of children out of birth;
the scarcely-noticed growth of
affection stronger than limbs;
cancer's surprise, or boredom's,
like pillowed halitosis;
an ageing belly heaving
from dried-out opposite—

Fifty years backwards, through astonished tears,
some old girls gave her a silver hockey stick
with names of distinguished pupils carved upon it.
To this, of course, no game could be attached.

One Day at Shieldaig. *Maurice Lindsay*

Behind rolled Vauxhall windows
two women, sealed in homely Aran sweaters,
knitted their fingers into sweated Arans.

Two men, cast off for
'a breath of air' (discretely to water themselves),
came sweating back, two strolling Arans homing.

Even the clouds and mountains
got knitted up in patterns of each other,
the sea's fingers glinting incredibly.

A Change of Fashion. *Maurice Lindsay*

On Summer holidays
my trouser turn-ups collected grains of sand,
pieces of shells and other memorabilia.

On earning days
I'd brush out these dried sights of sea and sky
to make way for the hairs of casual carpets.

You can't gather
capsuled space in trousers;
so now we've done away with turn-ups, and are
becoming less familiar with ourselves.

Hausfrau. *Suzan Livingstone*

Was darf es sein?
If only she guessed, behind her afternoon-tea face,
I want everything.
She thinks I want to buy a cream-cake—
Fifty seconds worth of compulsive calories.
I want everything.
She thinks I come to spend money
To buy her cloying chocolates.
I want everything.
She thinks I have everything,
But I have nothing—
  Just hausfrau
  Lonely hausfrau
  Bored hausfrau
  Fat hausfrau.

Summary. *Norman MacCaig*

In a quarter
of what I call my bones
a few mud huts are rising
to make a village.

In one of the parishes
of my eye, a flint
chips itself
into an arrowhead.

In a remote province of my mind
a wheel is invented,
dancing begins,
a man draws in a cave.

And in a dark corner
of my gut, another man
calls himself a priest.
God has discovered him.

What testaments he writes
of crucifixions, smouldering villages
and columns winding endlessly
into the future.

Patriot. *Norman MacCaig*

My only country
is six feet high
and whether I love it or not
I'll die
for its independence.

My Songs are Kandym in the Waste Land. *Hugh MacDiarmid*

Above all, I curse and strive to combat
The leper pearl of Capitalist culture
Which only tarnishes what it cannot lend
Its own superb lustre.

Somewhere in its creative faculty is concealed
A flaw, a senseless and wanton quality
That has no human answer.
An infernal void.

Capitalist culture to the great masses of mankind
Is like the exploitative handling in America
Of forest, grazing, and tilled lands
Which exaggerates floods and reduces
The dry-season flow of the rivers to almost nothing.

A hundred million acres, which might have maintained
A million families, utterly destroyed by water erosion,
Nine million acres destroyed by wind,
Hundreds of millions of acres more
Yielding rapidly to wind and water erosion,
Forests slashed to the quick
And the ground burned over,
Grazing lands turned into desert,
The tragic upsetting of the hydrologic cycle
Which has turned into disastrous run-off
The water that should have been held in the soil
To support vegetation and percolate
To the lower levels and feed wells and springs,
Till now the levee builders try to race
The Mississippi and set it up on stilts
Whence sooner or later it must stumble.
Problems of erosion control, regulation of river-flow,
Flood control, silt control, hydro-electric power.

I turn from this appalling spectacle
Of illimitable waste; and set myself, they say,
'*Gad im ghainims*' (putting a withy round sand).
The sand itself will produce a vegetation itself
If it is not interfered with. It will be a slow growth.
Nevertheless the vegetation manages to get a start
In the course of thousands of years,
And my poetry will be like the kandym
That doesn't advance step by step
But goes forward on the run, jumps through the air,
The little nut jumps along like a ball.
The sand comes along after, but the sand is heavier
And cannot catch up with the little nut
And bury it. But when the seed takes root
And the little shrub starts, the shrub
Cannot jump along like the seed ball.

How is it going to save itself
From the encroaching waves of sand?
It is not so easy to bury the kandym.
It doesn't have branches like those
Of the apricot and peach tree—its branches
Are slender and there are no leaves on them.
When the sand comes on the kandym doesn't try to stop it
But lets it go right through its branches,
Gives it right-of-way.
But sometimes the sand waves are so big
They bury the kandym nevertheless.
Then a race begins—the dune grows and the plant grows.
The dune grows fast but the plant grows faster still
And by the time the sand dune has attained its final height
The plant is found to have outstripped it.
Its little green bristles are waving in the wind
On the crest of the sand dune.
It has not only grown in height but has branched out too.

The whole dune is perforated with its branches.
The wave passes on, leaving behind
A good half of its sand.
So the little kandym has stopped the advance of the sand,
Turned the dune into a little hillock
Covered with vegetation.

But is there not one last danger?
The wind may blow the sand away
And leave the roots bare?
But the kandym knows how to fight with the wind too.
Lying flat in the sand it sends out extra roots
And holds the sand down with them.
In this way it gathers up the soil
And makes a foothold for itself.
My songs are kandym in the Waste Land.

Mexican Eagles. *Winifred Macdonald*

My Father once owned some Mexican Eagles.
From time to time he had news of them,
Printed in long columns which always tallied.
Often he would say 'I wonder how my eagles are today';
Or, looking up from his newspaper,
'Chris,' that was my Mother, 'my eagles are soaring.'
Sometimes he said, shaking his head,
'Those eagles will be the ruin of me.'

I'm glad I did not know
They were mere speculation in a foreign currency.
They soar throughout my childhood;
Or stand, great golden birds,
Shaking their shoulders in the sun of Mexico.

Or what else will it become? *Tom McGrath*

or what else will it become?

the child's tinkling
on a woolworth xylophone
plastic hammers on tin
see the cave and churchman
in the darker depths of skull
bird-skinned shaman part the flesh
pulse of wonder morning lights
the earth revives the xylophone
smoke roars in the hearth
in an elevator through the flames
trinkle trinkle remember monk

or what else will it become?

cat climbs up the window
squeaks the glass with his claws
get me out of my predicament
sleetfall on my fur gets cold
damp scratch miauing down the
pane
let me in
to the fire

or what else can it become?

well there goes the snow
or here it comes
a dance or downpour
downpuff cotton
the light is blue
cold flowers fall
well here comes the snow

or there it goes
the day will be picasso
black and white
ronepiped stark jawbone
in giant albino bull
of child fight dumpy man
with eyes of coal father
searching for his pipe
my day forever melting

here snows the go
or icicles run
stiff solitude

or, what else can it become?

an afternoon of jigsaws
jargon of the DJ show
apreslune de baudelaire
the prelude to a dawn
and foregone in the late-night
vaults I'll still be wondering
unstill wandering asleep and
raving till day breaks
resume my perch on edentree
cormorant spy on the new arrivals
stores up the data in an angeldevil mind
I am great dark seaoil crowned hooked
razorbeaked and wondering

Christ, what else will it become?

In Absentia. *Alastair Mackie*

'We've no heard frae God this while,'
said ane o' the angels.
It was at a synod
o' the metaphors.

Cam a wind;
it was a'body speirin'
'Wha?'
intill themsels.

It was heard by the sauls
o' Baudelaire and Pascal.
They fell through the muckle hole
opened by the question.

I' the boddom Jesus sweatit,
'Consummatum est.'
And Nietzsche,
hou he laucht and laucht.

The maist o' fowk bein' neither
philosophers or theologians
kept gaun tae the kirk.
Whiles, like.

Syne God said, 'Noo I'm awa,
mak a kirk or a mill o't.'
And God gaed tae the back o' beyond
i' the midst o' a'thing.

Pictures. *Menzies McKillop*

Pictures of galloping horses
In acres of boundless plains
Speak of gnawing people
On manioc, unhusked rice or mealies.

Similarly a raw boned quean
Streaming hair from a Jaguar
Argues a lack.

Young Girl. *Menzies McKillop*

The young heroes, the generous young men,
Wasting themselves like pennies at a wedding,
Will, when the sleep of exhaustion eludes them,
Think of her face.

Rams. *Alasdair MacLean*

Their horns are pure baroque,
as thick at the root as a man's wrist.
They have golden eyes and roman noses.
All the ewes love them.

They are well equipped to love back.
In their prime, they balance;

the sex at one end of their bodies
equalling the right to use it at the other.

When two of them come face to face,
in the mating season,
a spark jumps the gap.
Their heads drive forward like cannon balls.
Solid granite hills splinter into echoes.

They never wrestle, as stags and bulls do.
They slug it out. The hardest puncher wins.
Sometimes they back up so far for a blow
they lose sight of one another
and just start grazing.

They are infinitely and indefatatigably stupid.
You can rescue the same one
from the same bramble bush
fifty times.
Such a massive casing to guard a tiny brain!
As if Fort Knox were built to house a single penny.
But year by year those horns add growth.
The sex is outstripped in the end;
the balance tilts in the direction of the head.
I found a ram dead once.
It was trapped by the forefeet
in the dark water of a peatbog,
drowned before help could arrive
by the sheer weight of its skull.
Maiden ewes were grazing near it,
immune to its clangorous lust.
It knelt on the bank, hunched over its own image,
its great head buried in the great head facing it.
Its horns, going forward in the old way,
had battered through at last to the other side.

On Holiday in Ardnamurchan. *Alasdair MacLean*

No change. I find this land as hostile
as my forebears did before the navvies
drove their option through the hills.
My simple morning walk's resented here.
Wind and tide reach for my throat;
silence clings to me like brambles;

seaweed crosses rocks to trip me up
and judging by the way it hesitates
the path knows what's in store for us.
There's no appeasing such implacability.
I'd be a fool to try.   Even as I turn for home
a line of boulders closes ranks behind me
and the great sea-cave in Carraig Cliff
levels its black muzzle at my dwindling head
and fires a parting burst of pigeons.

Question and Answer. *Alasdair MacLean*

'Do you love me?   Do you love me?'
You keep on repeating the question.
'Say you love me.   I want to hear you say it.'
I say that once, when I was very young,
I saw a rat caught in a trap,
In a wire cage, squealing and snapping.
The cage was lowered into a tank of water.
I watched the stream of bubbles
slacken and at long last cease,
and when the cage was raised to the surface
the dead rat clung to the roof,
its jaws so firmly clamped around the wire
they had to be chiselled free.
But all this I say to myself;
to you I mouth, sullenly but truthfully,
the words you want to hear.
Satisfied then, you turn your back for sleep
and I lie awake, feeling the taste of the wire
between my teeth, feeling, in the darkness,
the cold water flow over me.

In the Evening. *Alasdair MacLean*

The light from the street shines in.
I stand at my window, my face
reflected in the glass. It rains,
streaming. My features trickle down.
The girl who lives across from me
has long blonde hair. Some nights
she sits there combing it for hours.
I wait. When she has finished I jerk
the curtains. The soft folds droop
before me. Darkness floods the room.

They show a film about Nuremberg
on television. Jackboots, swastikas,
sieg heils, the lot. I listen, trying
to follow the speakers. In the pauses
my blonde roar shakes the furniture.
My right arm is thrust upwards
and outwards, as rigid as an iron bar.
I can hold it this way for hours.

Fiona with a Fieldmouse. *Alasdair MacLean*

The grey thing
that scurries from my hayfork
I catch
and give into the cupped solemnity of Fiona,
who is three.
It is a thing so small
I could blow it out.
It is simply a tail hanging from a squeak,
a palpitation with fur round it.
Fiona has no words for it, no thought even.

She has narrowed her whole being
down to a pair of hands.
Never again in her life
will she achieve such concentration.
She will forget this moment
but it will stay with her
and what is piling up within it now
will periodically burst its banks
and come flooding over
husband, lover, child
or anyone lucky enough to be in the way.

Lunchbreak. *Gerald Mangan*

I didn't want coffee
but I've ordered it anyway;
there's a space left in my stomach.

It used to be morning rain,
and it'll soon be afternoon.
This always happens. I'm
filling in another hole.

I pour cellar-salt on coffee
-drips, and it turns brown, then
I form it into tiny cuboids, but
because these keep crumbling, it's
an endless process. You
have to do something, though.

I can't make a perfect cube of it, and
after all this work, obviously I can't
just flatten it with my thumb. I've
finished lunch and the coffee's
tepid; I ought to just go. But the

blonde opposite leans on long thighs
to fill her mirror, and trace her eyes,
and another doodles, blocks her O's—
I ought to just go; I spend my life
just filling in spaces.

Hotel des Invalides. *Gerald Mangan*

Her voice is in her shoulder-bag,
a ventriloquist's, tunnelling to fractured streets:
if it's older than Washington, she whispers, revere it.

Hens come out of roosts like this,
the twitch-round ruffling neck feathers, as if
expecting the arches to dine on her—
if you filmed her quickly, she'd vanish;
the negative would show the opposite wall.

And the cannon are trained on nothing
particular, and autumn's not choosy about falling,
but the way the negro rubs his blubbery
nape with empty tact, and the way the Citroën
2cv corners irreverently round the
courtyard cobbles, I start to say,
L'Europe aux anciens parapets, I'm here
in particular. You could photograph me.

But Paris some everyday morning is
here in general, is here in September, and fruit-
sellers grins I don't even notice when
the Seine blurs with rains of
ordinariness—and girls have lit cigarettes carefully
beside me before my awareness lights itself.

The Value of a Man. *John Manson*

If you do not want to think, say
He was always a bit that way.

His stock was rouped to pay a bill.
Did the agent lose his job for good?

Now he owns all the farms of the strath
And in their meritocratic way
The neighbours do not forget to ask him
About the crops and the animals.

What pay does he get at sale-days,
Dipping or threshing—union rate?

The shepherd seeks the one which is lost.
A man has no value.

Fisherman in his first year of Retirement. *A. S. Martin*

You wear what face furious time gave you;
it is a legacy, it is where history grew,
sown deeply by the hand of poverty, the hand of want.
So you give me your critical gaze as I invade your summer,
your only one. Can you sit now in
momentary sunlight and yet win shade and cool comfort,
away from a burning past which speaks in
strange hours of the massive facts you never questioned then:
hunger, and sleepless nights at home; and, at sea,
rapid journeys to the far brink of the herring's cycle?

Do you wince at a past which craves you, under
that saddened face, or, cushioned by a lack of guilt
rests beyond it all, beyond remembering,
locked in that terrible silence, unable to forgive?

Winter Fishing Off Arran. *A.S.Martin*

A chill wind stirs and coughs
mountains onto the land.
Silence. A heavy sky roofs
us over, jet-black, lined
with beads of simple light
where the quick rise
of the island merges into air.
The tongue too has its weight.
Ship passes ship in the dark. Our eyes
are absent to it all. The lights: green and red.
Engines stammer
apologies for our quiet; pound
the night to nothing. A streamer
of ocean falls off and unwinds
astern. We rock forward,
extravagantly, into the piled tides.

Gulls call and call and join
the ice, white, on the punishable decks.
Luck sides
with us. This is luck!
O lucky lucky men, we wait
too long and cannot look.
Dawn is it, or what?

The Green Room. *Paul Mills*

Raising the blind, she said—
'We like the landscape and the room
To blend.' The summer sunlight
Cushioned itself quietly
On the cooled surrounds.

Inside and outside—green, the carpet
Smoothed into a fitted lawn,
The walls into a costly screen of trees,
Beyond, the sea, kept at a distance
As colourless as sky.
'Even the weather'—I observed,

But watched the silence
Grow into disquiet, and wondered
How the trees behave, if at night
Something comes knocking

On the glass, or in the eye
Of a storm, if the white ornaments
Uncoil, fly into the static sea
Behind their heads, its huge walls
Of water about to burst.

The wind blew a clumsy leaf
Across the floor. 'Do you find what
You do rewarding then?'—she asked,
And did not taste rain in the teacup,
Her special blend, but drained
Into her skull, a second cup.

Now Afternoon. *Jean Milton*

now afternoon;   i polish silver with a
yellow cloth you sit silhouetted
against the faint sun shadow of window
transparent windmills lace curtains
tracingpaper
                    you paint a silvertipped bulb
lime green and orange.   A jar of lime water sits
by you.   The cat jumps the corks running to
crouch on your shoulder roaring its purr
from the depths of fur
                                        two goldfish float,
round the shells and blue marble in the jar.
Below them a bell dangles purple ribboned
from the red lamp and a winebottle's
shadow
            fronds of silk salmon shawl
trickle down the painted chair.
In the bulb's rounded silver i see myself
Convex Catlike Grinning
and as a magic witchball the entire room
whispering away

Goodbye to All. *Jean Milton*

GOODBYE to all the
stale fruitloaves
deepfrozen fish and chips
sponges like foamrubber
and tartan shortbread . . .
rows of sweet-filled jars i
drag down then heave up again
to the shelf;

idle hours i draw toffee
watery reflections on a tin;
the clock of the white church
is always two minutes fast;
the tea is always made from
a green packet with orange;
the empty Saturday afternoons
i spend talking to inside my
head looking at the hot sun
outside
          the sweet shop

Mr **.** *Jean Milton*

Mr **** stands motionlessly
anonymous
          (Polystyrene exhibit no.56)
outside the window waving a half-
opened tin of kitekat
                    dark sunglasses tweed
jacket furry trousers circa 1957
A grey figure, shoulders seen through a
split in the light diffusing tracing paper.
My head down, eyes follow up neck
                              head
                                  SHUDDER
down.
   we can't hear you SIR.

The Docks on Sunday. *Jean Milton*

the docks on Sunday

Hulks, ruined warehouses
echo the blasting radio from the hammer-tin
place across the estuary
The grasses blow, send their purple and white
crestfeathers floating
Sunny SUNDAY
Water moving, and I too
in imagined movement
THINGS
cold and bitter smell
of roasted iron and squashes boxes
rusty tins, bed springs
shadow on the melchy peat
NOISE
seagull cry.
The two walk on the dirty shore, crunch.
Blue trains run, clatters and squealing
bus brakes
CRACKING corrugated tin SHATTERING
foottrodden glass
waste dockland
Bagpipes shriek past the ricket remains of
wooden watchtowers, deserted tunnel domes
where glass was punched out and flowers float
out . . . out . . . out . . . out . . .

Afterwards. *Edwin Morgan*

Afterwards the sun shone on seven rice shoots and a black tree.

Afterwards the prostitutes fell on lean times / some took up embroidery / one became a pearl-diver and was drowned.

Afterwards my burned little cousin went through eleven grafting operations / never cried.

Afterwards many saffron robes began to be let out / there was a movement to purify the order.

Afterwards the ancient monuments were restored stone by stone / I thought it was folly when I saw the list of legless girls waiting for prosthetic appliances.

Afterwards there was a report of mass ghosts on the plains, all grey as dust, with grey shovels, burying and burying all through the night to the beat of a drum / but in the morning the earth was hard and unbroken.

Afterwards came six great harvests and a glut of fish, and the rivers rolled and steamed through tunnels of fresh green fruit-trees and lilypads needled by kingfishers / rainbow after rainbow plunged into the lakes of rice.

Afterwards I went out with my sister one still hot day into the forest, and we came to an old temple bombed to a shell, with weeds in its windows, and went in hand in hand through a deep rubble of stone and fragments of half-melted statues and rubbish of metal and flowers and bread, and there in a corner we saw the skeleton of a young boy, with shreds of blue cotton clinging to the bones, his fingers still clutching the string of a tiny bamboo box / we bent down as a faint chirping started from the box, and saw that it was his grasshopper, alive yet and scraping the only signal it knew from behind the bars of its cage / you said something and burst out crying / I slid the latch then and set it free.

The Milk-Cart. *Edwin Morgan*

Where are you in this darkness? I put out
a hand, the branch outside
touches only old October air
and loses leaves, it is hard
to wish for you, harder to sleep, useless to weep.
How can I bear the darkness empty
and how can the darkness bear love?

I bore the darkness lying still, thinking
that you were against my heart,
till I heard the milk-cart horse
come clattering down the hill
and the brash clear whistle
of the milk-boy dancing
on his frosty doorsteps,
uncaring as the morning star.
Come back to me—from anywhere, come back!
I'll see you standing in my door,
though the whistling fades to air.

At the Television Set. *Edwin Morgan*

Take care if you kiss me,
you know it doesn't die.
The lamplight reaches out, draws it
blandly—all of it—into fixity,
troops of blue shadows like the soundless gunfight,
yellow shadows like your cheek by the lamp
where you lie watching, half watching
between the yellow and the blue.
I half see you, half know you.
Take care if you turn now to face me.
For even in this room we are moving out through stars
and forms that never let us back, your hand
lying lightly on my thigh and my hand on your shoulder
are transfixed only there, not here.

What can you bear that would last
like a rock through cancer and white hair?

Yet it is not easy
to take stock of miseries
when the soft light flickers
along our arms in the stillness
where decisions are made.
You have to look at me,
and then it's time that falls
talking slowly to sleep.

Thoughts of a Module. *Edwin Morgan*

It is black so. There is that dust.
My ladder in light. What are my men.
One is foot down. That is pack drill.
Black what is vizor. A hiss I heard.
The talks go up. Clump now but float.
Is a jump near. A camera paced out.
I phase another man. Another man is second.
Second last feet on. The dust I think.
So some soles cross. Is a flag near.
No move yon flag. Which voice comes down.
White house thanks all. Command module man except.
Is kangaroo hop around. I think moon dance.
Or white bird is. Good oxygen I heard.
Earth monitors must be. Is it too pressing.
Trained man is gay. Fail safe is gay.
The black I see. What instruments are lonely.
Sharp is a shadow. A horizon goes flat.
All rock are samples. Dust taken I think.
Is bright my leg. In what sun yonder.
An end I think. How my men go.
The talks come down. The ladder I shake.
To leave that bright. Space dark I see.
Is my men last. Men are that first.
That moon is there. They have some dust.
Is home they know. Blue earth I think.
I lift I see. It is that command.
My men go back. I leave that there.
It is bright so.

Whooops! I nearly smiled again . . . *Pete Morgan*

'Whooops! I nearly smiled again,'
said the King to the Harlequin,
'My enemies draw closer
our ranks are wearing thin
but that was very funny—
what you told to me before—
the one about the monument
and the man who shouted "More".'

'Your Fencibles have fallen,'
said the Herald to the King,
'The drawbridge has been taken
and there is one other thing
the Queen has gone to Galahad
and your pioneers no doubt
are picking up the pieces
of the Army put to rout.'

'Whooops! I nearly smiled again.'
said the King to the Harlequin,
'This sad affray is ended
there is no kith to my kin
but that was very funny—
all my subjects died in style
I lost my crown, my mace, my spurs—
I almost had to smile.'

'Yes,' I said 'but is it Art?'. *Pete Morgan*

Took me to the battlefront
  saw the mushroom cloud
said 'We can see the colours even
  when our heads are bowed.'
Showed me the destruction
  the slaughter a la carte
said 'Isn't Nature wonderful.'
  'Yes,' I said
  'but is it Art?'

Took me to the scientist
  opened up a phial
said 'This is only chicken-pox
  and rhino bile.'
Showed me what it did to mice
  said 'That's just a start
but isn't Nature wonderful.'
  'Yes,' I said
  'but is it Art?'

Took me to the hospital
  pulled aside the sheet
said 'Look at that pulsating
  listen to the beat.'
Showed me the incision
  threw away the heart
said 'Isn't Nature wonderful.'
  'Yes,' I said
  'but is it Art?'

Took me to the tenement
  knocked on every door
said 'Have you see the copulation

practised by the poor?
We select the ones to breed
and we reject a part
but isn't Nature wonderful.'
'Yes,' I said
'but is it Art?'

Took me to the prison
threw away the key
said 'If you learn our lesson
you could still be free.'
Pointed out the spy holes
and my adaptation chart
said 'Isn't Nature Wonderful?'

'Yes,' I said.

Elegy for Arthur Prance. *Pete Morgan*
The Man Who Taught The Stars To Dance.

The toes that tapped through morning air
were once stand-ins for Fred Astaire.
The heels cool in the gutter where
the dancer lies up-ended.

The one time only Arthur Prance—
'The Man Who Taught The Stars To Dance'—
had reached his zenith with a jig
which once came over very big
on radio.

The feet that clicked from ten flights high
and danced flamenco down the sky
had once made Ginger Rogers cry
'His *entrechat* is splendid.'

The one time only Arthur Prance—
'The Man Who Taught The Stars To Dance'—
possessed an act of wide appeal
especially his eightsome reel
danced alone.

The one time only Arthur Prance—
'The Man Who Taught The Stars To Dance'—
performed his final pirouette
and heard applause he didn't get.

One of them was Washing. *Pete Morgan*

One of them was washing '*His*' body in Milk

One of them was washing '*His*' body in Milk
he trembled
he was endlessly whistling
& continually repeating to himself
Milk . . . Milk . . .
Good Milk
& he wanted very much to become clean.
He had two hands
and a quantity of Milk
which he carefully rubbed
into '*His*' body.
He paid particular attention to
'*His*' body
& he wanted very much to become clean.
He stood trembling
in the centre of the room
and carefully dried '*His*' white body
repeating to himself
Milk . . . Milk . . .
Good Milk
& he wanted very much to become clean.

The Salt Sun. *David Morrison*

We came upon the sea by chance.
Waves did not roll onto the shore.
Huge rocks slept, sizzling
In the salt sun.

Lines of seaweed swarmed and crawled.
Under the boot, small pods cracked.
Great trees lay, half under the sand,
White, and well seasoned
For the coming sculptor.

We came upon the sea by chance;
No sound warned the ear.
On such a day
The sea slept in the sun.

Herb Robert. *Angus Murray*

Cold on the rock, in the sun's glance
pink at the final burst
Impious and Uncertain like Chance
or the footsteps of assassins in the shadow,
the hangman's white apprentice at the first
dangling
through the lattice-work of grasses
by the river; careless with its graces
like the tinker suddenly emerging
from sleep and city park
into the street of many faces
clean and questioning.

If I like he emerge, abide
in some remote and alien plane; along
the rich banks of Heaven's side
I'll see
by my God or where it be
an Isis far from crumbling pyramids of Nile
the pink Herb Robert covering every mile.

Frost Round The House. *Anne B. Murray*

There is no sound under the frost.
Tonight it is as though the walls are frozen too
So intense is this silence, this stillness.
Nothing moves at all
And I wonder,
What sounds usually fill the evenings
When winter and darkness bend houses to the earth?
Usually there is sound or I wouldn't notice the lack.
There is no creak of a robbing wind unwary on rafters
No sound of a window's struggle.
There is no murmur from outside from the deeps of the tumbled burn
No muted mutter of trees and waves.
There is no sound.
All round the house the night sits hunched as an owl
Feathered and still
But more still than the night,
Inside the house
Is the curious listening of the air—
Yet
There is no sound to hear.

Two Branches. *Anne B. Murray*

Time has gone
Out of autumn
And now
I hold in my hands
Only the wrinkled berries
Of a day
Of wind.
Shriven, dry
They lie in my hands,
Smaller than before
The leaves without life.
I hold also
A branch
That is all thorns
And that is
As it was.

Primates! *Edward Borland Ramsay*

The grey sloth of night
creeps into my being,
numbing for a time
all sense of supremacy!
The mind clings to the bough of
sleep! Eyelids flicker, diffuse light
like will-o-wisps! I am barely conscious
of the Primates!

Von Braun. *Alexander Scott*

1. You built the *Apollos*
from London bones.

2. Your hypodermic stabbed space
and drew blood.

3. Was Cain the captain
who read us *Genesis* round the moon!

4. Killing creator,
breath to a dead world.

5. Whose bones will we bury
to grace it green?

Scotched. *Alexander Scott*
A Selection from *A Sequence of Scarts*

1. *Scotch God*
Kent His
Faither.

2. *Scotch Religion*
Damn
Aa.

6. *Scotch Education*
I tellt ye
I tellt ye.

8. *Scotch Queers*
Wha peys wha
—For what?

9. *Scotch Prostitution*
Dear,
Dear.

22. *Scotch Presbyterianism*
Blue
Do.

23. *Scotch Glasgow-Irish*
God
Weirs a green jersey.

24. *Scotch Orangeman*
Bully
For Billy.

26. *Scotch Liberty*
Agree
Wi me.

27. *Scotch Equality*
Kaa the feet frae
Thon big bastard.

28. *Scotch Fraternity*
Our mob uses
The same razor.

32. *Scotch Optimism*
Through a gless,
Darkly.

33. *Scotch Pessimism*
Fient the
Gless.

34. *Scotch Modernity*
Auld
Lang syne.

35. *Scotch Initiative*
Eftir
You.

36. *Scotch Generosity*
Eftir
Me.

37. *Scotch Co-operation*
Pou thegither
—My wey.

38. *Scotch Geniuses*
Deid
—Or damned.

Gentlemen prefer Blondes. *Alexander Scott*

Is tha' a fac'?
Nae broun or black?
Nae reid? Nae mous?
Nae gowd, nae use?

Wha says? Wha kens?
Whas judgin, men's?
Wha's feart o't, quines?
Wha's yours? Wha's mines?

Wha daurs? Wha dwaums?
Wha sings them psalms?
Wha pents them pure?
Wha harles them hure?

Wha dees? Wha dyes?
Wha lees and lies?
Wha blesses bleach?
Whas law? Whas breach?

Wha's richt? Wha's wrang?
Wha gilded gang?
Wha's fair? Wha's foul?
Whas gowden rule?

The Straits. *Valerie Simmons*

If I stare at you,
driving slate seas,
it is because I want to draw from you
all your loveliness into my own face.

I gave away the rare colours
I got from the sea-anemone,
and the stippled sheen
from a mackerel stiffening.

Strength was a beauty I thieved
out of the line of the moorland;
—regard its breaking
over the prominences of his skull
like the watershed of the high ridge.

His eyes,
spaced well apart,
have no pupils,
are broken windmills
slipping a hold
on the cliffs of air,
missing,
missing in rhythm.

The god had shins
like a cutting edge,
and I reached for them
never thinking
to be left with no hands.

The place is
solitary,
lain on my back on the night shore,
knobbed spine fits the pebble crevices.

From across the straits
a little rain comes
to lay the dust.

Chaplin. *Iain Crichton Smith*

Everything seems pasted on,
the baggy trousers, the moustache.
The teeth shine over a smashed dish.
The silence helps him. Watch his pose,
the v-shaped broken boots. The doors
swing shut to hide him. He fights
the moving elevators,
cycling upstream.
His cane is thin as a stem.
One could not lean on it. He pulls
thick cultures down. He trudges on
to a thriving emptiness.

Garbo. *Iain Crichton Smith*

She is walking away from somewhere in her long coat.
You see her at the end of avenues, like a lot
in which she once enacted others.
The street
takes her away as at a film's end. That, she can't
wholly escape—her past which is made of light.
In an absence of music her dark glasses look, once.
Then, slowly, she turns away, furred in her silence.

End of Schooldays. *Iain Crichton Smith*

Captains, this is your last day in school.
You won't wear these helmets any more.
Do you not hear the whisper in the triumph,
like a suspect heart? Do you not see
how Mr Scott, though kind, is harried
by voices inaudibly calling from his house.

Look out on the fields. Never again will you see
such a sweet greenness, as of colours leaving
a place where they've been happy for a while.
The harness is turning now to other horses.
Laughter comes up the road and mounts the brae.
The names on the doors are rewriting themselves.

Never mind, the music will not leave you
or not completely. Sometimes in a betrayal,
in the middle of a deal just turning rancid,
after the fifth gin, the fifth fat hand,
the cloudy globes, set on the cloth, you'll hear it,

the music of your Ideal, quietly humming
in locker-rooms that smell of sweat and rain.
You'll be coming home in a warm and eerie light,
legs tall and willowy, in your hand the cup,
shaking a little, in your flabby hand
the trembling cup, in your old grasping hand.

Return. *Iain Crichton Smith*

I lived in that room fifteen years ago
high above the roses. I see a maid
moving in white beyond the pale window.
Strangers own it now and a wooden sign
swings to and fro, swings endlessly to and fro,

saying 'Bed and Breakfast'. 'Vacancy'. It was
a time I have forgotten. Better forget.
The lights turn elsewhere now. And the tall stairs
creak to the English visitors who bring
their happy Easter faces to the north.

We change. All changes. As I turn away
there's a wedding on, just at the small church there.
New children bend after old pennies.
A door bangs shut. A black car slides away
in snowflakes flung from open gloved hands.

Opposite it, the mill is still standing.
Black pails, brown pipes, new planks and knotted wood.
The sawdust rises, wave on wave, like meal.
My arm aches for a plane, a saw, a hammer,
for anything solid in the sparkling stream.

This is the Time of Darkness. *Iain Crichton Smith*

This is the time of darkness. Everything falls,
cigarettes and matches, needles and vodka, everything.
When you walk the street, houses are clumsy and gray,
moustaches are painted on people, and the booming Colonels
with the voices of foghorns rise out of tweed and stone.

This is the time of darkness. Walk under ladders
and surely the paint will splash you. Surely the ashtrays
will fall on the point of the joke. Surely your dress
will split in the moonlight, neat as the halves of an orange.
The phone rings on and on in an empty house.

These are essential sorrows, I see you ascending
through strata of rocks, through iron, through a writhing of worms.
The bulbs cast their schoolgirl pallor, black beaks are sounding
the depths of the earth. Punctual, accurate, perfect,
dressed for your party in yellow, you're ready, bright Ceres.

I saw the Mune. *Sydney Goodsir Smith*

I saw the mune at nune the day
Blue sky and sun and the mune there tae
It was the morning and the evening baith thegither
It's aye the mornin and the eenin baith thegither
  —For us.

At the last day
As at the first.

  But this, hairtbeat,
  Is bang in the middle
  And wants nae bush—
  Nae mair nor gowden wine does
  Or a broch around the mune
    That says:
  . . . . .Rain. . . . . .rain. . . . .

Rain, beat doun
And raise the gowden corn again;
Sun, sheen on, all orient,
First day and last;
Mune, sheen—
The mornin and the eenin baith thegither.

In the rule o' the sun brairs the corn,
Sweys in the souch o' the wind
Like the souch o' the swaw in the faur-aff sea,
The mune ascendant—
Her dominion there . . . Selanna!
Venus . . . Ceres . . . Pluvius . . .
  Names, juist names—
Sol and Luna there conjoined
  —Juist names.
    Names.

But though we name auld names, my maisters,
Calling the past to clout wir raggit coats
And decorate a platitude auld when God was a laddie,
Think nocht tis idle sherbet that we sup
In this Sicilian idolatrie—

Aa kens, nae need here to repeat,
There's millions on the earth has gods nor meat;
Thousands ligg in chains and need
For nocht but speakin freedom's leid.

In aa this waesomeness and want
Guilt for love were piddling cant.
Act, gin ye will, act and move!
But speak nae word except ye love
—Or, humbug, let me see ye staund
And cast the first stane frae your haund.

Here we love, remote and safe,
And cry that love is unity—
Aa lovers think they hae it baith
Though the earth quags beneath their feet.

I saw the mune at nune the day,
Blue sky and sun—
      A memorie.

Winter. *Sydney Goodsir Smith*

The trees naked in the streets—
A deein sun dwynes 'gallantly in splendour' in the west
  (War lord stuff!)
The luift hammered, bruished to rose and royal purple;
Wee skitterie raggit clouds
Like young Valkyrie streamin hame
Swift as hunting dugs across
The tall gray lands o' Reekie—
  Stane and bluid, bluid and stane.
  A parable, a history.

It was a sicht, I'll tell ye,
Without the word o'a lie
  —Says Bob the barman
  Snug in his steamin howff,
  'Oblivious o' the finer shades', of course—
  But wyce, withal.

All nature croodles doun for the lang nicht;
The auld wounds greit in the cauld
  (As Jimmie, auld sodger, kens fou fine
  Wi's steel shin and back o' solid siller—
  A warrior—Salute him!)
The winter season o' cauld, as the auld bards cried it . . .

The seas run black in lumps in the haaf;
The fine snaw blinns the ee;
Boats run for harbourie;
Landwart fowk under roof—
Coal to the fire.

And there, on younder tree
A single leaf,
Ae leaf alane on a bare tree
  Hingin, juist—
The endmaist finger-touch o' life
Secure in its ain essence
  (Its leafness, as auld Scotus said)
But no secure at all, as ye ken—
Na me, na you, lass that fills my hairt.

But here it is, my love—hear this:
Though leaf nor tree nor earth kens ocht,
Or the wheeling winds that lift the sea,
There's this I say to thee in love
And stupid parable and simple leid:
The tree that draps the endmaist leaf
Readies its cap for the new spring green.

For us the winter seas o' the hairt
Break green on green—and white at last.

Autumn Haiku. *Alan Spence*

damp leaves
drift
to earth/the
sun hangs tangled
in the branches
of a tree.

Winter Haiku. *Alan Spence*

fresh-fallen show,
not yet trodden by
anyone's feet—
I'll charge across!

A Cold Snap. *Robert Tait*

Something has snapped.
Could it be the chemical bond between
sugar and spice and all things nice?
Something has occurred to me,
that I haven't run into you lately /
That still waters don't run deep either
                                        they're in chunks /
that I've been saving up for a rainy day
                                        in a week of sleet /
that you led me up the garden path /
that winter may already have you too
                                        in its grip /
that you don't grow on trees
                                        any more than money /
that I've lost even the path
                                        in the garden /
that everything snapped
                                        this minute when I saw you:

distant as a street photographer's target /
distant as a smile on a billboard /
distant as flowers in a winter garden /
distant as Mao's era of a thousand blooms /
distant as Cuba and India /
for which sugar and spice too
are so absurdly homesick.

Annalisa. *Robert Tait*

She's full of energies that collide inside
  her and knock her about.
She's like a little old-fashioned aeroplane
  with a semi-transparent body
  and an engine making it shudder.
  In a dogfight you worry about that flimsy rudder,
  everything sounding off at once all over her,
  strung like with piano wires,
  exhaust farting.
She's full of steam then tears,
  drying in her own wind,
  hands fluttering like propellers
  hedge-hopping the chairs.
She's like a little old-fashioned aeroplane
  because she's only three
  and we
  look back at her through time;
  so what we see as she pulls
  up a steep incline from our shops is that
She's fuming and sparking with quick hatreds, quick
  rolls of her eyes to be quit of us, quick
  sorties, unafraid and intact, between keystone cop
  cars, quick invasions of our privacies indoors,
quick switches from ugliness to a shape we can take
  and want, won't stay put, retreats far
  into sleep, leaving us further up in our creepy
  lumbering jumbo jet, pitched high
  on that powerful, irresistible, unending, tied note.

The Director writes to His Girl. *Robert Tait*

I'm sending you the shots
of us together, with love.

Funny how we're never
in the one frame, though.

Deep down I say, 'But we
were shot together,

Film doesn't behave like quicksilver,
nor do we, rolling

apart at a touch, at a glance.'
But there it is.

I've riddled the screen with holes.
My camera blows apart.

I'm smoking nervously,
or my gun is. Love.

P.S. What were we discussing anyway?
Being together, dying together or revolutions?

You remember you had a fear of my camera,
called it my cold tool, then froze.

I think the poor thing was helpless then,
and that it's just too passive to lie.

No You. *Robert Tait*

No you can't
have a close-circuit television
showing a brothel of all-blond negresses /
No you can't
pee and expect wine even if you are drunk /
No you can't see my heart /
No you can't
be allowed to come here with flowers
even if you do love me /
No I won't have you
invite Dr Christian Barnard to my next
birthday party, I see through you,
and you won't get to my heart that way /
No don't think I'll let you
away with writing letters on condition
that you stay in Naples
while I research the correspondence
of Thomas Carlyle /
No you can't see
the proofs, they're confidential /
No you can't,
the executors have an embargo on their love
letters, no you can't just /
you don't think you can simply /
you surely don't imagine /
you're not just going /
to catch that bus, are you?

Woman is. *Anne Thomson*

A woman is as free
who brings each purpose
to another's sharing.

A woman is as wide
who evolves in the distance
between kindred events.

A woman is as wise
whose folds are collecting
the dust of her knowledge.

A woman is as cruel
whose weapons are hammered
to shape on mind's anvil.

A woman is as giving
who swings close, secured,
with the gifts of ancients.

A woman is as naked
whose garments hang limp
in the halls of the faithless.

Renewal. *Anne Thomson*

this is the
gift
renewed

windfall
of
fruit

from
unreachable
branches

a small
patch of
earth

stained
by its
juices

oozing from
broken
skin.

Second Time Around. *Anne Thomson*

you have been
left reflector
on some
forgotten
circus that folded
up
months ago the
costumes shabby sequined
glitter the acts
haphazard
go to hell in
stupid oblivion
lets all choose
our
transport.

Suicide 2. *Gavin Trevelyan*

am I male or female
why does she keep sewing blue buttons on my white shirts
if I dont do something those boys will never learn to make
their heads
the car was too hot and full of dust
white on the red seats and red dash-board
the trees dark-green where their colour could be seen
covering of white dust
we saw an elephant
how big
his eyes were red as far as I could see
thc boys said they saw them grey
if only we had a colour film
if only she would sew properly
they say that women who cant sew are dependent on their mothers
well I wouldnt like to be dependent on her
theres money there
a better house
with more garden
if I dont do something Im going to do something
every day I expect that every day
and it just doesnt
last year when they went on holiday I was going to get out
then the girl got ill and I had to hold the telegram
if I dont do something those boys will never learn to make
their heads

A Sea-Girl's Cry. *Valda Trevlyn*

Grey granite, not black diorite as in Lenin's tomb
But the blue slate of Delabole,
Gold shelving sands and gorse,
Cold blue of the sea,
Warm blue of the skies,
Downs spattered with purple thyme,
Sand-dunes sweating with the prickly heat of sea-holly;
The quick speech of the womenfolk,
The men slow-blooded with their broad lazy drawl.

Coast-wise the gay little boats
(I'm thinking of Mevagissey),
Painted in senna, blue, green, and red,
The Liza Jane bold in black and white, the hussy,
Riding the harbour's swell.
When I think of the North—Bude, my home-town—
It's the waves rolling and folding in,
The breakers we call them
Then roughing up and battering
Against the breakwater.
Sharp toothed rocks, blue with mussels, limpet-studded.
The Whale's Back and Compass point
I scrambled about as a young girl
Crying to the wind—there was always a wind,
How I loved that Cornish wind!

And Morwenstow—Hawker's hut—
Where I led a slow boy on and ditched him,
Holsworthy Fair, and my first love
Racing the sands at midnight
Calling it Jordan—why?
The sound of the sea sloughing out to the tide-line,
Wet sand under our feet,

The wind in our hair, and laughter—
   Everything for free.
The laughter I miss most of all.

I climbed Rough Tor and Brown Willy
And the world was at my feet,
I wanted to fly with the wind
   Over the hills and far away.
   One day I did just that.
Now I'm old and it's crying time,
But the memories of Spring days
   Will never be forgotten,
Now like a ship that sails on the night-tide
   And on that ship's wake
   My thoughts reach back.
Now I know what you mean to me,
   Cornwall—too late!

Granite City Eclogue. *Roderick Watson*

Shines like frost   quartz hard   is worked with difficulty.

Perdurable.   A source of pride in character and action
is in that glittering obduracy of mind   formidable
as Annie Davidson   —a relative 16 years dead
and not far removed   —who left service
as a lady's maid   by plaiting her employer's braids
into the back of the bedroom chair   and slapped her face
carefully   —had six children (and five survived).
Her life's pride   was always to have managed.

But if endurance is a virtue   it makes us accomplice
to suffering   and its verity a convenient motto
for the merchant fathers   who made more hose
out of less wool   by observing   what the girls wasted
at the end of the factory day   and stopping it.
For the men of standing   who built grace into Grecian banks
and baronial hotels   and for the owners in their time
the elders of the steam trawler   in quiet houses
with sweet gardens   risen   from the fish
the stink of the catch   silver   on rusted plating
dredged out of the North Sea   cold   blooded   teeming
the coin of that round and ruptured eye   bright as mica

exploding in the pan   brought in by the ton
on deck with frozen hands   split raw salt flesh
weeks out for days in town   drinking   fucking
spending   sick as a cat in the lavvie   and out for more
two suits on the door   Sunday shoes under the bed.
For fish does not last   at all   and ripeness counts
and people have to manage   and damned if they don't.

Little virtue then   in such prideful exercise of grip
and scorn for what doesn't hold   and little ease
in the hard word.   Nevertheless   I value true things
by their difficulty   —a resistance to the will—
and celebrate this desperate intransigence   in all creation:
for   at the last   I cannot credit grace
among accomplishments   in place of what is *here* and *endures*
nor deny the stern fathers   the merchant men
their inheritance   without accepting too
that ecstasy of opposition   which is how the son begins.

Defined by indirections   I am here
in the blossom of Cambridge   and away from home   mostly.

Welthistorische Perspektiven. *Roderick Watson*
for Marlene Dietrich

Her face with bones
like Dresden china,
a hollow look
over leather gloves
and sequins on the back:

Siren eyes
for Paramount Pictures,
black, black.

reflects a park in flames
trees like the rim of a sun,
the green houses crazed
and peacocks
that could not fly;

Coronas!
Run, run,
from the sky.

remembers the lines
of men at the railway
and women in queues
for bread
in the streets.

After that Winter
Spring came
a bitter green.

Dim as cigarette smoke,
with her hat and beaded veil
over ash blonde hair,
she takes the glass from her lips
leaving the rim stained red

A girl
must pay respect
to the dead.

and calls them up, the old songs
drowned voices on record,
pleading in the attic
from cold earphones.
Messerschmitts call in the air.

Home to stay.
We'll meet again,
somewhere, somewhere.

Footnote If read aloud, *Welthistorische Perspektiven* is intended for two voices reading simultaneously, so that the lines opposite each other coincide in timing and delivery. Thus, 'like Dresden china' and 'Siren eyes' should *chime* together, like a chord where separate notes make a new single resonance.

Springsong. *Roderick Watson*

When the winds of March and April's rain
brought the year into Spring
and at dawn the butcher heard
the first and sinister cuckoo call,
   he took his wife to hand
twice   hard on the bloodstained planks
at the back of the market stall,
   before the early customer
before the shocked sheep-eyes
                                        Rise up and do observance.

Then Madam Nature stands downtown
at the gate of the garden of love
in an apron swinging keys,
she delays those who presume
   to come upon Venus at noon
and her green-apple breasts;
or Criseide with red hair
   –a sparrow on a thread
eating crumbs from her moist palm
                                        Lovers pay respect and more.

When things must start again
and the old in one another's fields
stoop over their bags of seed
before the labour of a sowing;
   to tramp in one more year
of coarse flour and plain tack
they intend no less
   than to bring bread
out of stones
                                        Rise up and do observance.

Then matrons at their washing
whisper of the wolf
seen at the market cross,
or why the wheelwright killed his girl
   with a spokeshave to her throat;
and of the lord's own son
with his peacock hose and dagger slung
   –held by a silk cord
between such tight bright legs
                    Lovers pay respect and more.

When the damned in his cell
sees her face turn again
into the light   into a mask
only he and the gargoyle know
   because of her ways in a darkened shed
and a spokeshave from behind;
the priest comes to show him peace
   and how to use his time
with beads   before he hangs
                    Rise up and do observance.

Then   at last   the butcher leaves
his wife alone with the flesh,
and walks to Castle Hill
with a bag and a bottle of red in his hand
   to string the gibbet there:
then flowers bloom in gold leaf
and birds parade in rings
upon the littered ground,
   and then the lascivious fly drones
and the horned snail sings   *Now*
                    Lovers pay respect and more.

True History on the Walls. *Roderick Watson*

You cannot get away   from what has gone before

Cut back   even to Agamemnon's men   dug in
between the unsown fields   fighting for Troy
in mud and leather armour   boastful:
and the corroded blade   turned over in the soil
so thin   among the pebbles of a broken mound
like an old nail.   Or the bound man at the peat-moss
who was ploughed in like dragon's teeth   to secure
the richness of the ground   but rose again
at Tollund fen   with the seeds still in his belly.

Black wire   barbed at every inch   coils
in the sand like a tapeworm   you cannot get away:
your cut foot jumps in my hand   and I watch
how the blood falls   and turns to small round stones
rolling on the leeward slope of the dune.
Clumsy—will these grains burst at my touch
and bleed again?   (The concrete bunkers on the beach
are foul with piss and excrement   scratches
on the walls inside   form words in the light
that shafts from each slit   obscenity   broken
bones   rusted tins   you cannot get away)
Cut back.

To the faces in the family album   —like these two
gathered in stiff clothes   and committed to memory:
she died   and at the back of the book
this man killed her   (effectively responsible)
with the seventh child of his unemployment.
There is no print of them together   at the marriage
of their histories   (pressure and resistance)
they are figures in a hereditary landscape   and yet
they will come back   reduced   but still returning.

Repetitious as the heroes with dry palms rubbed thin
as old paper scaling on lampshades who sit
on the park bench discussing the damp and how
it kills you grips the liver like claws and painful
to pass water at times. Old wounds. From a great night
three years ago god the days we knew then
fighting them off (we were) on hands and knees
behind the door porcelain to the forehead cool
embraced so comforting when the saliva runs
paper towels cold water nor may you escape
the consequence. (Cider bottles to reclaim
in the morning back at the grocer's again).

Pressure and resistance. Between the point
that bears in and the blue dimple held
before the skin breaks and the whole story
is made known. You started to cry in the kitchen
and I—having driven you there—regretted it
among the bright boxes and the plates laid out
came then to give comfort (action/reaction)
and you asked quietly that I leave you alone.
Cut back. It is within us all the old history
and no escape from the bones of our fathers
(the corroded blade turned over) or the cruel
fascination of their true ends.

–Which lean upon us like the wind
on the road bridge walking that afternoon
with the sun caught in the high towers and you
unsure of the water like hammered glass so far
down and the running clouds that make the bridge
seem to fall slipping sideways out of the sky
(seven men died in its construction).
We were balanced between shores (pressure
and resistance) as delicately as sea gulls planed
on the updraughts below us and some hope in this

for such skill   and beauty also   comes back
as our wounds do from what is passed   yet remade
minute by minute: a mending of the distance
between us
(and you cannot get too far away.)

Reading Room. *Heather Wood*

The boy opposite me
Has long fluffy hair and a beard
The colour of mustard
Sticking out round his head
Like a sacred fungus.

He wears a blue floral tie,
His eyes are staring, like blue daisies.
From time to time
He breathes sharply and jerks his ballpoint
In pretended annoyance.

When the man brings his books
The boy is careful not to look up
Or say thanks.
He is pregnant with the image of himself
And must protect it.

Sailor's Epitaph. *Heather Wood*

White swans, white swans,
Who will sail with me to England?
England is locked,
The key is broken
Sand is stifling—
And bells are pealing.

Notes *on some of the Contributors*

D. M. Black, b. 1941, Wynberg, S. Africa.
With Decorum, Lowestoft, Suffolk 1967. *The Educators*, London 1969.

Alan Bold, b. 1943, Edinburgh. Poet and freelance journalist.
Society Inebrious, Edinburgh 1965. *The Voyage*, Edinburgh 1966. *To Find the New*, London 1967. *A Perpetual Motion Machine*, London 1969. *The State of the Nation*, London 1969. *A Pint of Bitter*, London 1970.

Derek Bowman, b. 1931, Liverpool. Lecturer in German, Edinburgh University.
Translator of *The Life Story and Real Adventures of the Poor Man of Toggenburg* by Ulrich Bräker, Edinburgh 1970.

George Bruce, b. 1909, Fraserburgh. Writer.
Sea Talk, Glasgow 1944. *Scottish Sculpture* (with T. S. Halliday), Dundee 1946. *Selected Poems*, Edinburgh 1947. *The Scottish Literary Revival, an anthology*, London 1968. *Poems 1939–70*, Edinburgh (in press).

Thomas A. Clark, b. 1944, Greenock. Writer.
The Secrecy of the Totally, Sherborne, Dorset 1970. *Down and Out in Tighnabruaich*, Preston 1970. *The North Bohemian Coalfields*, Bettiscombe Press 1970.

Stewart Conn, b. 1936, Glasgow. B B C Radio Drama Producer.
The Chinese Tower, Edinburgh 1967. *Thunder in the Air*, Preston 1967. *Stoats in the Sunlight*, London 1968.

Robin Fulton, b. 1937, Arran. Writer's Fellowship at Edinburgh University, 1969–71.
An Italian Quartet, London 1966. *Instances*, Edinburgh 1967. *Blok's 'Twelve'*, Preston 1968. *Inventories*, Thurso 1969. Editor of *Lines Review*, Edinburgh.

Robert Garioch (Sutherland), b. 1909, Edinburgh, 'Lexicographer's orraman'.
17 Poems for 6d., Edinburgh 1940. *Chuckies on the Cairn*, Edinburgh 1949. *The Masque of Edinburgh*, Edinburgh 1954. *George Buchanan's Jephthah and The Baptist Translatit in Scots*, Edinburgh 1959. *Selected Poems*, Edinburgh 1966. *The Big Music*, Thurso (in preparation).

Duncan Glen, b. 1933, Cambuslang. Head of Graphic Design, School of Art, Preston.
Hugh MacDiarmid and the Scottish Renaissance, Edinburgh 1964. *Stanes: a twalsome of poems*, Kinglassie 1966. *Idols*, Preston 1967. *A Sunny Summer Afternoon in the Park?*, Preston 1969. *Kythings and other poems*, Thurso 1969. *A Small Press and Hugh MacDiarmid*, Preston 1970. Editor of *Akros Magazine* (1965–), Preston. Editor of *Selected Essays of Hugh MacDiarmid*, London 1969.

Giles Gordon, b. 1940, Edinburgh. Publisher.
Two and Two Make One, Preston 1966. *Two Elegies*, London 1968. *Pictures from an exhibition*, London 1970. *Eight Poems for Gareth*, Frensham 1970.

G. Andrew Greig, b.1951, Stirling. Salmon fisherman; writer.

Robin Hamilton, b.1947, Kilmarnock. Student.

Roderick Hart, b.1944, Methlick, Aberdeenshire. Teacher of English.

Alan Jackson, b.1938. Writer.
Underwater Wedding, Edinburgh 1961. *Sixpenny Poems*, Bristol 1962. *Well Ye Ken Noo*, Bristol 1963. *All Fall Down*, Edinburgh 1965. *The Worstest Beast*, Edinburgh 1967. *The Grim Wayfarer*, London 1969.

Peter Jamieson, Lerwick. Journalist and author.
Letters on Shetland, Edinburgh 1948. Founder/editor of *The New Shetlander*, Lerwick.

William Keys, b.1928, Glasgow. Teacher of English.

Colin Kirkwood, b.1944, Edinburgh. Area Principal for Adult Education, Derbyshire.

Tom Leonard, b.1944, Glasgow. Publisher's reader.
6 Glasgow Poems, Glasgow 1969. *A Priest came on at Merkland Street*, Glasgow 1970.

Maurice Lindsay, b.1918, Glasgow. Director of the Scottish Civic Trust.
Perhaps Tomorrow, Oxford 1941. *Predicament*, Oxford 1942. *No Crown for Laughter*, London 1943. *The Enemies of Love*, Glasgow 1946. *Hurlygush*, Edinburgh 1948. *At the Wood's Edge*, Edinburgh 1950. *Ode for St Andrews Night and Other Poems*, Edinburgh 1951. *The Exiled Heart*, London 1957. *Snow Warning*, London 1962. *One Later Day*, London 1964. *This Business of Living*, Preston 1969. *The Lowlands of Scotland : Glasgow and the North*, London 1953. *The Lowlands of Scotland : Edinburgh and the South*, London 1956. *Robert Burns ; the Man : his Work : the Legend*, London 1954. *Clyde Waters : Variations on a Theme of Pleasure*, London 1958. *By Yon Bonnie Banks : A Gallimaufry*, London 1959. Editor (with introduction): *John Davidson : A Selection of his Poems*, with preface by T. S. Eliot and Essay by Hugh MacDiarmid, London 1961. *The Discovery of Scotland : The Accounts of Travellers from the 13th to the 18th centuries*, London 1964. Etc., etc.

Suzan Livingstone, b.1938, Whitehaven. Teacher of backward children.

Norman MacCaig, b.1910, Edinburgh. Lecturer at Stirling University.
Far Cry, London 1943. *The Inward Eye*, London 1946. *Riding Lights*, London 1955. *The Sinai Sort*, London 1957. *A Common Grace*, London 1960. *A Round of Applause*, London 1962. *Measures*, London 1965. *Surroundings*, London 1966. *Rings on a Tree*, London 1968. *A Man in My Position*, London 1969.

Christopher Murray Grieve ('Hugh MacDiarmid'), b.1892, Langholm. Author and journalist.
Sangschaw, Edinburgh 1925. *Penny Wheep*, Edinburgh 1926. *A Drunk Man looks at the Thistle*, Edinburgh 1926. *First Hymn to Lenin*, London 1931. *Lucky Poet*, London 1943. *Collected Poems*, New York 1962. *Selected Essays*, London 1969. Etc., etc.

Winifred Elizabeth Macdonald, b. 1912, Grangemouth. Free-lance writer.

Tom McGrath, b.1940, Rutherglen, 'Explorer'.
My Love Stop Is Stop, London 1970–1.

Alastair Webster Mackie, b.1925, Aberdeen. Schoolteacher.
Soundings, Preston 1966.

Menzies McKillop, b.1929, Oban. Schoolteacher.
Poems (Parklands Poets No. 3), Preston 1969.

Alasdair Maclean, b.1926, Glasgow. Schoolteacher.

John Manson, b.1932, Gills, Caithness. Teacher.
Editor (with David Craig) of *Hugh MacDiarmid : Selected Poems*, Harmondsworth 1970.

A. S. Martin, b.1952, Campbeltown. Editor of local weekly newspaper.

Paul Mills, b.1948, Cheshire.

Edwin Morgan, b.1920, Glasgow. Senior Lecturer in English, Glasgow University.
Beowulf : A Verse Translation into Modern English, Aldington 1952. *The Cape of Good Hope*, n.p. 1955. *Poems from Eugenio Montale*, Reading 1959. *Sovpoems*, Worcester 1961. Editor: *Collins Albatross Book of Longer Poems*, London and Glasgow 1963. *Starryveldt*, Frauenfeld, Switzerland 1965. *Emergent Poems*, Stuttgart 1967. *The Second Life*, Edinburgh 1968. *Gnomes*, Preston 1968. *Proverbfolder*, Bath 1969. Editor of *Penguin New English Dramatists 14*, Harmondsworth 1970. *Twelve Songs*, West Linton 1970. *The Horseman's Word*, Preston 1970.

Pete Morgan, b.1939, Leigh, Lancashire. Writer.
A Big Hat or What?, Edinburgh 1968. *Loss of Two Anchors*, Edinburgh 1970.

David Morrison, b.1941, Glasgow. Deputy County Librarian, Caithness.
The Saxon Toon, Edinburgh 1966. *The White Hind*, Thurso 1969.

Anne B. Murray, b.1932, Scotland. Physiotherapist.

Edward Borland Ramsay, b.1913, Rutherglen. Barber.

Alexander Scott, b.1920, Aberdeen. Senior Lecturer in Scottish Literature, Glasgow University.
Prometheus 48, Aberdeen 1948. *The Latest in Elegies*, Glasgow 1949. *Selected Poems*, Edinburgh 1950. *Untrue Thomas*, Glasgow 1952. *Mouth Music*, Edinburgh 1954. *Shetland Yarn*, London 1954. *Still Life : William Soutar*, Edinburgh 1958. *Cantrips*, Preston 1968.

Valerie R. Simmons, b.1948, Alberta. Student.

Iain Crichton Smith, b.1928, Isle of Lewis. Schoolteacher.
Thistles and Roses, London 1961. *The Law and the Grace*, London 1965. *From Bourgeois Land*, London 1968. *Consider the Lilies*, London 1968. *The Last Summer*, London 1969. *Survival Without Error*, London 1970.

Sydney Goodsir Smith, b.1915, Wellington, New Zealand. 'General literary hack.'
The Deevil's Waltz, Glasgow 1946. *Under the Eildon Tree*, Edinburgh 1954. *So late into the Nigit*, London 1952. *Omens*, Edinburgh 1954. *Figs and Thistles*, Edinburgh 1959. *The Vision of the Prodigal Son*, Edinburgh 1960. *Kynd Kittock's Land*, Edinburgh 1965. *Fifteen Poems and a Play*, Edinburgh 1969. *Collected Poems*, Edinburgh (in preparation). *Carotid Cornucopius*, Edinburgh 1964. *The Wallace*, Edinburgh 1660. *Full Circle* or *The Stick Up*, Edinburgh 1969. Etc., etc.

Alan Spence, b.1947, Glasgow, 'Various'.
Plop!—15 haiku, Glasgow 1970.

Robert Tait, b.1943, Kilmarnock. Editor of *Scottish International Review*.

Anne Thomson, b.1950, Lanarkshire. Clerk.
The Glimpse I Give You, Glasgow 1969.

Gavin Trevelyan, b.1943, South Africa. Student.

Valda Trevlyn, b.1906, Bude, North Cornwall. Housewife.

Roderick Watson, b.1943, Aberdeen. Research student.
28 Poems (with James Rankin), Aberdeen 1964. *Poems* (Parklands Poets No. 7), Preston 1970.

Heather Wood, b.1945, Aberdeen. Research linguist.
A New Grammar of Modern Frisian (in preparation).

Postscript

Over the past few years an increasing number of poems submitted and accepted for *Scottish Poetry* have had longer lines than those published in previous numbers. To accommodate this change *Scottish Poetry 5* has been given a new shape.

The Editors acknowledge their debt to *Akros*, *Lines Review*, *The New Edinburgh Review* and *The Scotsman* from which some of the poems were selected. The majority of the poems in this anthology were submitted by the poets themselves.

The Editors continue to welcome new poems from Scottish writers.